A Guide to Getting It:

A Clear, Compelling Vision

Teresa Aziam • Michele Corey
Diane Cunningham • Fran Fisher
Michele Molitor • Sharon Nichols
Claudette Rowley • Vanessa Sandarusi
Marilyn Schwader • Linda Snyder

Marilyn Schwader, Editor

CLARITY OF VISION PUBLISHING • PORTLAND, OREGON

Other books in the series:
A Guide to Getting It: Self-Esteem
A Guide to Getting It: Achieving Abundance
A Guide to Getting It: Remarkable Management Skills

For more information, visit www.ClarityOfVision.com
To order any of the *A Guide to Getting It* book series, visit www.AGuideToGettingIt.com

BOOK DESIGN AND PRODUCTION BY MARILYN SCHWADER

ISBN 0-9716712-3-0
Library of Congress Control Number: 2002116109
First edition: December 2002

Table of Contents

Acknowledgements v

A Note from the Editor vii

A Vision From the Heart by Marilyn Schwader 1
   Vision and Living in the Moment 3
   Vision and Dreaming 6
   Vision and Choice 9
   Vision and Obstacles, Hurdles, and Setbacks 11
   Vision and Purpose 12
   Allowing the Vision to Unfold 13

Let Your Vision Find You by Sharon Nichols 17
   Start Where You Are 22
   Start a Life Portfolio 24
   Start With Support 28

Inner Pathways to Vision: Five Ways to Move Beyond Your Barriers
   by Claudette Rowley 33
   What is a Compelling Vision? 34
   My Inner What? 34
   Five Pathways to Listening to Your Inner Voice 35
      Tap Into Your Heart's Wisdom 35
      Connect With Your Body 35
      Listen to Your Intuition 36
      Notice Your Self-Saboteur 36
      Identify Limiting Beliefs 37
   You Get to Want What You Want 38
   Signs That You Are On the Right Path 39
   Vision-Stoppers 40
   Mobilizing Fear to Your Advantage 41
   Vision Building 42
   Vision Expansion vs. Release 44
   Messages From Your Inner Voice 44
   What Are Your Undreamed Dreams? 45
   What's the Life You Would LOVE to Live Right Now? 46

Living Your Vision® ~ From the Inside Out by Fran Fisher 49
   Step One. Discover: Who Am I? (Inside Out) 54
   Step Two. Clarify: What Do I Want? (Inside Out) 56
   Step Three. Create a Plan (Inside Out) 57
   Step Four. Work My Plan (Inside Out) 58
   Step Five. Review My Plan Routinely (Inside Out) 60
   Step Six. Utilize Support 60
   Miracles 63

Are Your Limiting Beliefs Affecting Your Vision? by Diane Cunningham .. 69
    How Do You Recognize Limiting Beliefs? 71
    Where Do Limiting Beliefs Come From? 74
    How Do We Change Limiting Beliefs? 75
    Belief Audit 77
    Secondary Gain 83

Moving Beyond Fear to Find Your Vision by Michele Molitor 87
    Inspiration from Al 87
    Moving Through the Fear 88
    Values as Building Blocks 89
    Values vs. Fear 92
    The Power of Perspective 94
    Breaking Free 96
    Freedom of Choice 99
    What's at Stake? 100
    How do You Find Your Vision? 101

Live Life More Fully With a Vision by Linda Snyder 105
    Your Life Reflects Your Thinking 106
    Motivations for Change 108
    What's Stopping You From Living Your Vision? 110
    From "What" to "How" via "Why" 112
    Visualizing Your Life 113
    Self-Talk 114
    When to Start Creating Your Vision 116

A Journey to Re-discovering Your Authentic Self by Michele Corey 121
    "It's Happening" Alerts 131
    The Foundation 132

What You See is What You Get by Vanessa Sandarusi 139
    Identify Your Needs 141
    Living In Integrity 143
    Now Look at What You Want 144
    Using Your Intuition 145
    Take Action Steps 149

Maintaining Your Vision, No Matter What Happens! by Teresa Aziam 155
    What is Your Dream? Defining Your Vision 155
    Be Aware of the Beliefs That Affect You 156
    What Are You Hiding Under That Basket? 158
    Don't Be Afraid to be Where You Are 159
    Keeping an Eye on Your Intention 160
    Do What You Can One Step at a Time 161
    Be Your Own Best Balcony Person 163
    Don't Let Others Make Their Experience Yours 164
    Be Proud of Your Dream 165
    Keep Going. Even If It Seems Like It Will
    Take Forever to Reach the Top 165

Acknowledgements

For many years, the idea of having a clear, compelling vision has fascinated me. Realizing that coaching helped clarify my client's vision, I even named my company Clarity of Vision. There are so many people that have encouraged me to create the life of my dreams. I thank them for being there as guideposts and sounding boards. In particular, I thank the coaches who have contributed their knowledge and experience in the writing of this book. They have helped me fulfill my vision, and for that I will always be grateful!

Marilyn Schwader, Editor

A Note from the Editor

The pages in this book comprise a unique guide that will allow you to gain access to powerful, life-changing insights, examples, and exercises to help you create a clear, compelling vision for your life. As you will find in reading the chapters in this book, your choice of picking this book up is just the first step to manifesting that vision.

As you read these pages, be prepared to re-discover your dreams and desires, to see how you can have the kind of life you've always hoped for, and to discover ways to put the ideas presented into motion. Creating your vision is one of the greatest journeys you will undertake in your lifetime. Use this book as your map, your Guide to your Clear, Compelling Vision!

This book is the fourth book in a series of books written by Life and Business Coaches to help the reader improve their business and personal life. I invite you to read, explore, and enjoy!

Marilyn Schwader, Editor

A Vision From the Heart

By Marilyn Schwader

Several years ago, while searching for the next path on which my life would take me, I went home to visit my parents for an extended stay. After experiencing job burnout, I was ready to stop working for someone else and to start something of my own. When I was a child, my parents had taken me to a restaurant/nightclub that my cousin, Ray, owned. Ray was a large man, with a pot-belly and a substantial presence. His establishment was known throughout eastern South Dakota and people traveled hours to come to the steakhouse for dinner and dancing. Ray lived large, and people seemed to gravitate to him. I thought to myself that owning a restaurant was a great occupation and I decided that someday I wanted to own one myself. I had a very glamorous perception of what it would be like to be socializing with patrons and of the attention Ray seemed to receive. The seed was planted and I dreamed of one day owning a restaurant.

On my visit to see my folks, my parents and I were returning from an evening out when my mother asked if I had decided what I was going to do next in my life. I proposed to them my dream of owning a restaurant. My dad replied, "Why in the world would you want to do something like that? I can't see why anyone would want to own a restaurant." Although I had heard the phrase from him before with my older siblings, hearing it in regards to my dream was disheartening. We pulled into the garage, and after he went into the house, I asked my mom why he was so discouraging. She said, "Don't you realize that when he says that, he's not talking about you? What he's really saying is that *he* wouldn't want to own a restaurant. Don't let his view of the world keep you from having your own dream." The moment was a turning point for me.

In the days after my mom shared her insight, I felt an awakening. I realized that I had spent the previous five years traveling a path that had been for someone else. I had stopped dreaming about what I wanted to accomplish, and had focused on externals—the money, the things I could buy, the prestige of doing the work I was engaged in—in the hopes that those things would make me happy. But I hadn't been content for a long time. In the weeks since I had left my job, I hadn't really spent any time searching for what I *wanted* to do. My time had been focused on what I *should* do.

I started to expand my dream of the restaurant and began to envision the colors of the rooms, what pictures would hang on the wall, and how the food would look on the dinnerware. I began to design the menu and imagined the taste and smell of the food. I decided that the restaurant would have separate rooms, each with its own theme, and I picked the music I would play in each of those rooms. I started to write lists of things I would need to research and searched for recipes that I might use. Although I had no idea where I would find the financing, I felt that somehow I could make it happen.

When I returned home a week later, I had a complete picture in mind. And suddenly things started appearing that seemed to illuminate that I was on the right path. I found a book on the Middle Ages, an interest of mine, and when I opened the book a poem about owning a tavern appeared. A friend—who didn't know of my dream—called to invite me to meet a friend, who turned out to be a chef. She introduced me to a consultant who not only helped me open the restaurant, but who became my first chef. Everything fell into place, and those obstacles that would have seemed insurmountable a month prior, seemed smaller somehow. I was in a flow, and the universe responded. Within a year, the restaurant opened. I had created my vision, my dream.

Within five years, the restaurant was closed.

There are many reasons that I could point to that would explain why the restaurant failed. In fact, for some time, I blamed just about everything for my lack of success: I chose the wrong business partner, I didn't do my due diligence concerning legal aspects of the lease, my good friend and chef left due to personal reasons, and on and on. But when all is said and done, the underlying reason was that when I had accomplished my vision, I stopped dreaming. I stopped imagining the next place I wanted to be moving toward.

So let me take you on a journey. First, to that place where dreams develop, then down the path that will take you to where your dream becomes reality. And know that the journey never ends. Every day is a winding road and at each bend, another set of crossroads will appear that will require you to keep expanding that vision, to make choices and embrace change so that you can continue to be inspired and passionate about where you are, and where you are going. To have a clear, compelling vision that propels you forward through obstacles, hurdles, and setbacks, so that you can live life fully and with enthusiasm.

Vision and Living in the Moment

"The light from one small moment of honest self-inquiry is more powerful than the accumulated darkness of a million years of doubt." ~ Guy Finley

In his book, *Design Your Destiny*, Guy Finley says that, "Each of us is created with the power to choose our course of destiny." To be able to do this, you must first learn how to access the place where your future is being created: the present moment. The concept of the present moment, while hard to grasp and live in, has complete power over what happens in our future. That moment is our destiny, the meeting of who (our being) and what (our nature) we are.

The force that unites these two parts of our destiny is self-awareness.

How can living in the moment and creating a vision—which seems like a far-off point in time—be mutually dependent? Being in the present moment means that you are not thinking about regrets over something that happened in the past. Nor are you thinking about what might happen in the next moment. You are, without thinking, *experiencing* the feelings, sights, and sounds within and around you right now. This state of self-awareness is the same as the moment in which you just became aware. If you are truly in the present moment, within your being, you won't be thinking about which direction is best for you. You won't have to choose from the old patterns that produce limited beliefs. New alternatives will appear as your inner vision. These messages from your true being will guide you.

Let me tell you a story of how I discovered the true sense of living in the moment. A few years ago, I went on a weeklong raft trip down the Rogue River in southern Oregon. As we were putting the six-person rafts into the river, the guide asked if anyone would like to take the trip in an inflatable kayak. Never having tried it before, I decided to give it a go. The first leg of the trip was relatively calm, with a couple of class two rapids, so I was able to get a feel for the craft and the river before we headed into more significant whitewater. At one point, I found myself caught in a small eddy, a river current at variance with the main current that causes a whirlpool-like effect in the river. I struggled to paddle out of the eddy, and when I finally pulled away, found myself floating backward down some rapids. I began to panic. I am a strong person, but was unable to bring the kayak around to face down river. Fortunately, the current carried me up against a medium-sized rock. From there, I was able to push off of the rock and bring myself around in the right direction. At the next still water, I paddled to the edge of the river and caught my breath.

In those moments—which seemed like an eternity—I had an epiphany. Being on the river was like paddling through life. As the current carried me, I realized that to safely navigate the channels and rapids that I would encounter, I needed to be fully present. I might have a few seconds to make a decision about a direction to take, but ultimately the current would take me where it wanted. The more I struggled with the direction I wanted to take, the more difficult the trip became. When I stayed in the moment, trusting that I would make the decision necessary at the point I needed to, I began to see the entire river more clearly. I began to see how the water broke against the rocks and how the current changed directions. Staying in the flow instead of resisting its direction gave me a sense of calm, even in the class four rapids we encountered later down the river. What control I had was limited by the power of the current as it channeled through the canyons and over the rocks. The more I fought the flow, the less success I had and the more effort I had to expend. The river became my guide, just as my creative self guides me when I am present and in the moment.

"THE INTELLECT HAS LITTLE TO DO ON THE ROAD TO DISCOVERY. THERE COMES A LEAP IN CONSCIOUSNESS, CALL IT INTUITION OR WHAT YOU WILL, AND THE SOLUTION COMES TO YOU, AND YOU DON'T KNOW HOW OR WHY." ~ ALBERT EINSTEIN

In the present moment you merge with your self-expression. You don't question your next move, or your choices, or what the results will be in the end. You are in the natural flow. When this happens, all of your experiences are affected. You will know what you need to know, when you need to know it. As Penney Peirce says in her book, *The Intuitive Way*, "When you are in the present moment, the question and answer always exist together and arise in the same instant. Trusting this implicitly, solutions may not fit your expectations, and experiences are no longer right or wrong—they're just right." You will not have to *think* about your vision; it will come to you.

As your trust in the moment increases, you begin to experience less anxiety about the past and the future, and are more in tune with your surroundings. There's synchronicity. Inspiration and enthusiasm increase, and as they do, you feel happier. When you are happy, you become more spontaneous, creative, and productive.

This is not to say that we should ignore action and achievements. Doing and having, as well as being, are a part of the creative process. Logic, goal-setting, and management of objectives is important. However, the first step is to be self-aware, which expands your understanding and provides more clarity of the process. Then you can begin to streamline objectives, which ultimately brings more enjoyment to each task and accomplishment.

Vision and Dreaming

"The door to the world is the heart." ~ Coreta Kent

My family plays a game. We don't have a name for it, but here's how it's played. Each person describes another person in the family with only one adjective. As you might guess, this game reveals much, both about the describer and who they're describing. The words my family uses to describe me are usually pretty similar: optimist, idealist, enthusiast. And most of all, the word used is dreamer.

Like many people, for years I believed that being a dreamer was a bad thing. We are all allowed to dream when we are children. Adults ask who you want to be and the sky is the limit. I wanted to be an astronaut, an oceanographer, an actress, a singer, and an artist. As I entered my adolescence, those same adults who encouraged my dreams when I was five began to question those very same dreams. Eventually, I learned that being too "out there" with my dreams would sometimes bring derision and ridicule. So, I began to adjust my dreams to conform to "reality."

The next step to creating your vision is to learn to dream again, to "think" with your heart, to reestablish your connection with your creative being. Think about a time when you lost yourself in a hobby or activity, when time seemed to float by without thought. I can spend hours in a bookstore or in nature finding new trails to explore, and can lose myself in my garden. When I am in those spaces, I'm honoring my creative self. I feel alive, refreshed, and ready to tackle other pursuits.

When I ignore my need for these creative endeavors, I will eventually be reminded by my creative inner voice that my heart is wanting. This manifests in different ways, but most often by pain and discomfort. And if I wait too long, life hits me over the head with a big life lesson.

How can you get back to that childlike dreaming place? There are a couple of ways that I will suggest. One is to do a dream wheel. I recently created my dream wheel, and it immediately took me back to pre-school days. Your way of doing this exercise is entirely up to you. You can use materials you have on hand, or you can have fun collecting the items. I went to an art store and purchased some sparkling gel pens in a variety of colors and some large sheets of colorful pressboard. Then I went to the bookstore and visited their magazine section. I chose magazines with pictures and images that I felt reflected what I want in life: Natural Home, Backpacker, House Beautiful, Sports Car, Whitewater Paddling, Outside, Fine Gardening, Travel & Leisure, Outdoor Photography, Islands, etc.

I chose pictures from those magazines that reflected things I want in my life, places I want to go, and things I want to do. Then I drew a large circle on one of the pieces of pressboard and divided the circle into the following categories: Home, Relationship, Vacation, Mind, Business, Play, Spiritual, and Photography. I glued the pictures that related to each area into the area of the wheel that they fit. I hung the wheel on my bedroom wall, and can view it every night before I go to sleep and every morning upon waking.

The process did two things for me. First, it allowed me to think in pictures. Visionaries in any field will tell you that they think in pictures. People use mental imagery every day. In business it might be in flowcharts, in design work it might be using picture boards. The person creates an image of what he or she would like the outcome to look like. The dream wheel provides this imagery in a tangible way.

Second, it gave me a tool to bring those images to my subconscious. Once an idea is in the subconscious, the mind and body begin to find ways to manifest that into daily life.

The second exercise I will suggest is to think back to your childhood. On a piece of paper write down the answers to these questions:

- What fascinated you as a child?
- What did you daydream about?
- What did you love to do as a child?
- What secret fantasies did you have?

Write the answers, no matter how silly or unimportant they seem to you right now. Don't limit yourself or make judgements about your answers. Have fun and just write. Take the time to daydream, to fantasize again, to imagine all of the possibilities. Stay present with the process, imagining what each activity felt like, how your senses were filled in the activity.

One result of the process of learning how to dream again is that we rediscover who we are at our base. This sounds like a simple concept, but for most of us, in our hectic lives, we've lost this most important piece of the picture.

Again, there seems to be a contradiction with staying in the present moment and dreaming or thinking about the fantasies we might have had as a child. Remember, when you do these exercises, do them without expectations, regret, or judgement. Just *be* with the dream. You are creating your vision and your destiny in this moment. Embrace it and love it, and trust that what you find in the process is what you need for the next moment.

Vision and Choice

"Be careful what you set your heart on, for it will surely be yours." ~ Ralph Waldo Emerson

I enjoy walking. I try to do it every day, as it quiets my mind and acts as a form of meditation for me, and I usually come away from the walk with at least one new perspective, if not many.

During some of the most difficult days operating the restaurant, as I was struggling with the choices I had made, and what I might do differently, I went for a walk on an old logging road in the forests near my home. The day was dreary and rainy, and my mood wasn't much better. As I climbed yet another hill, the sun broke through the clouds and sent a ray of light down on both the path in front of me and on a large Douglas fir tree that stood in the middle of a fork in the road. As I stopped to admire the sight, it reminded me of an image that I had thought of frequently in my search for why I had made the choices I had made, and where those choices had taken me. The image was of a crossroads where there were signs pointed in many directions, with different mileage for each destination. There were always dozens of choices and each time I saw the image, I also saw myself frozen with indecision.

For the first time in years, as I stood at that fork in the road, I was in the moment. And in that moment I saw myself at the crossroads again. Only this time, I suddenly had the understanding that staying there struggling with my decisions would not take me anywhere better. While I had the choice to stay there and live with the decisions I had made, I also could pick any of the possible destinations and at least take one step toward a new place. If it led me down a path that might not be any better than where I was, I realized that I could make another choice to change to another direction. At least I would be taking action, instead of being stuck.

I had for so long been in overwhelm that I had not done anything to change it. I did manage to worry myself into ill health, to procrastinate with details, to exhaust myself with anxiety. What I realized was that I wasn't overwhelmed with the unending list of things to do, but the presence of the *thought* that the list was unending. All I was seeing was the number of things that I needed to take care of and how difficult it was to choose what to do next, instead of picking one and moving in that direction.

If the vision that you have for your life isn't working for you any more, you can change it. When you are faced with so many tasks that you think you won't be able to finish them in your lifetime, make them more attainable by writing each one out on a piece of paper. Don't put them in any order of importance. Just write them down. Your priorities will only be as clear as your thinking, and this exercise helps clarify both.

Now take the first item on your list and get that thing done. When finished, take the next thing and do it. Looking at the entire list will paralyze you. However, when you take one thing at a time, you will be able to accomplish it.

You can choose to deal with what is in your power—or with what isn't. When you waste your time on things that aren't in your power, you give them a life that they wouldn't otherwise have. So, you don't need the strength to deal with what's been defeating you, you only need the understanding that it can be removed from your life. The power you have is to choose to let the old thought go and get back to allowing your new vision to come to you.

In the universe of imagination, there is no limit. However, in the physical world, gravity, space, and time bind us. Choice is the bridge that connects your creative spirit with "reality." Making one decision at a time, putting one foot in front of the other, your choices create the tapestry that is your life. You are the sum of your choices. And nothing you envision will manifest unless you can say *yes* to this and *no* to that.

Vision and Obstacles, Hurdles, and Setbacks

"Nothing you're afraid of losing can ever be the source of your fearlessness." ~ Guy Finley

One of the most important reasons for having a clear, compelling vision is that it is what leads us to overcome enormous obstacles and setbacks. When I had the vision of the restaurant in my mind, and I felt in the flow and knew the reasons why I was moving toward that end, the hurdles shrunk and setbacks didn't seem overwhelming.

However, my mistake was that once I had accomplished that one vision, I didn't have another vision of what the restaurant would be and how my life would look five years down the road. Without that new vision, I was thrown out of the flow and nothing was compelling me to overcome the obstacles that kept appearing. With an image in mind of what I wanted, barriers had seemed surmountable. Without the vision, the image of how large those obstacles were crowded my mind. The presence of the *thought* that they were insurmountable kept me from conquering them.

Take a moment to imagine in taste, touch, sound, smell, and sight every detail of an activity that you enjoy. For example, if it's painting a picture, imagine the feel of the canvas, the smell of the paint, the environment you've created around you, the music you listen to as you paint. Now imagine an activity you don't like, like driving in heavy traffic. Again, think of the same senses you experienced doing that activity.

While thinking about driving in traffic, re-create the sensations of painting that you had and overlay those onto the new activity. Imagine that driving is as satisfying and interesting as painting. Do this while you are driving and you will soon discover that you forget about the driving, and become more calm and at peace.

In the same way, once you have created a clear, compelling vision, imagine what that place will feel like to all of your senses, and those things that seem to get in the way will shrink in their importance. You will feel more tranquil and at ease as you proceed toward that vision.

Vision and Purpose

"The oldest wisdom in the world tells us we can consciously unite with the divine while in this body; for this man is really born. If he misses his destiny, Nature is not in a hurry; she will catch him up someday, and compel him to fulfill her secret purpose."
~ Sarvepalli Radhakrishnan (president of India, 1962-67)

Several months ago, I was talking with my coach about my business. In an attempt to help me clarify my vision, she asked what I felt my purpose for my business was. I responded by saying that I had difficulty answering that because I was still questioning my purpose in life, much less my business! I have felt all my life that I have an important reason for being here; I just hadn't been able to discover what it is that I'm meant to "do."

Since I work from a home office, I'm usually very disciplined about the time I spend "at work." The day after my coach and I talked, as I struggled with the idea of finding my purpose, I found myself unable to concentrate on my writing. I decided to do something different. I went downstairs to my "play room," thinking I would work out while watching some afternoon television. I pushed the "On" button and the first image I saw was Oprah introducing her guest for the day. She said, "Today I'd like to welcome our guest Caroline Myss, who will be discussing her new book, *Sacred Contracts*, which describes how we can find our purpose in life."

The universe had my attention. I watched the show as I worked out, and that night went to the bookstore and purchased the book. Myss proposes that we don't really have to "find our purpose" because we are already living our purpose. We make choices and decisions in the manner we do because they are fulfilling our "...Sacred Contract—the guided plan for our life." A Sacred Contract represents the "earthly commitments, the tasks you have been assigned, and the lessons you agreed to learn in this incarnation in order to fulfill your divine potential."

Learning to trust that every action I have taken—and will take—is simply fulfilling my purpose gave me a tremendous sense of calm. The saying "Everything happens for a reason," which I had heard for years, suddenly made complete sense. Letting go of the idea that I had any "control" about where my life was taking me gave me an immense sense of relief. Trusting the moment, living in that present state, I see my purpose every day. This makes a huge difference in how I approach people and events, because now I believe that every encounter, every action, every decision I make is living my purpose. That being the case, I want to be sure that all of those moments are lived with the fullest intention that they are fulfilling my purpose and taking me one step closer to living my vision.

Allowing the Vision to Unfold

"LOVE WHAT YOU ARE DOING AND NEVER BE AFRAID TO FOLLOW WHERE YOUR NEXT IDEA WILL LEAD." ~ CHARLES EAMES

Allowing your vision to unfold requires that you live your present life with awareness. When you pay attention you will see the messages and opportunities that will take you in the direction of your vision. As you finish this book on creating a clear, compelling vision, you might be feeling an urgency to get started, to strategize, plan, and control the outcome. The process doesn't work that way. Creating your vision follows the language of your heart, which is not linear, rational, or predictable. Like a river, your heart has its own rhythm and momentum. Embrace your dream, stay alert, and be ready when the door of opportunity knocks.

As you proceed down the river of life, you may encounter eddies in the current and obstacles hidden in the water. To navigate the channels, let go of how your dream will come about. A vision from the heart will take on its physical form in ways that are unpredictable and uncontrolled. Like the raindrops that become the streams that flow into the river, each step in creating your vision builds on the one before. Open your heart to see your vision, and when you do, you'll know your destiny.

"AND NOW HERE IS MY SECRET, A VERY SIMPLE SECRET; IT IS ONLY WITH THE HEART THAT ONE CAN SEE RIGHTLY; WHAT IS ESSENTIAL IS INVISIBLE TO THE EYE." ~ ANTOINE DE SAINT-EXUPERY

References

Capacchione, Lucia. *Visioning: Ten Steps to Designing the Life of Your Dreams*, New York: Penguin Putnam, Inc., 2000.

Finley, Guy. *Design Your Destiny,* St. Paul: Llewellyn Publications, 1999.

Gottlieb, Annie, Barbara Sher. *Wishcraft: How to Get What You Really Want*, New York: Ballantine Books, 1986.

Myss, Caroline. *Sacred Contracts: Awakening Your Divine Potential*, New York: Harmony Books, 2002.

Peirce, Penney. *The Intuitive Way: A Guide to Living From Inner Wisdom*, Hillsboro, Oregon: Beyond Words Pub Co., 1997.

About
Marilyn Schwader

As a Writing and Life Coach, Marilyn uses humor, compassion, and a strong sense of a writer's abilities to support and motivate her clients to become published authors. She has found that her purpose in life is to give a voice to subjects that benefit others. Her mission is to provide truthful, clear, and motivating information to those who passionately desire more in their lives. Her vision is to use her two passions—coaching and storytelling—to convey this information to as many people as possible.

Marilyn graduated from Oregon State University in Corvallis, Oregon with a Bachelor of Science degree in Technical Journalism with emphasis in Business Management. After working for several years as a technical writer contracting to high tech companies in the United States and Pacific Rim countries, she veered from the writing path and started her first business, M's Tea & Coffee House, in Corvallis.

Five years and numerous disastrous business mistakes later, she left the restaurant business and a short time later discovered Coaching. In 1998 she enrolled in Coach University and started Clarity of Vision, a Business and Life Coaching practice. The law of attraction soon worked its magic, and her talents and experience in writing soon began drawing writing clients to her business.

During this time, Marilyn undertook a three-year project to compile and publish a book about her mother's family history. From that experience, she began helping people self-publish their books. Looking for a way to combine her coaching and writing experience, Marilyn decided to create a book series that would be written by coaches and that highlighted principles and ideas supported in the coaching process.

Thus, the *A Guide to Getting It* book series was born. *A Guide to Getting It: A Clear, Compelling Vision* is the fourth book in the series. *A Guide to Getting It: Self-Esteem* was published in January 2002; *A Guide to Getting It: Achieving Abundance* in August 2002; and *A Guide to Getting It: Remarkable Management Skills* in October 2002.

For more information about Clarity of Vision Publishing, visit www.ClarityOfVision.com. To find out more about the *A Guide to Getting It* book series, visit www.AGuideToGettingIt.com. To contact Marilyn, send an email to Marilyn@ClarityOfVision.com or call 503-460-0014.

Let Your Vision Find You

By Sharon Nichols

A couple of years ago, my husband Scott and I were madly packing boxes and orchestrating a major summer long transition. There was so much to do! We were moving out of our home, putting most of our life in storage, packing luggage for a month in Italy, making arrangements to house sit after we returned, setting aside yet more stuff we'd need when we got back, and assembling a portable office to keep my business mobile until we eventually got settled. It was crazy! For weeks, my life was dictated by a several page to-do list that I affectionately called "The Motherlode." Managing all of those details was a lot of work. But it was also very exciting. We were making these changes because one of Scott's dreams was finally taking shape.

Several years earlier Scott had received his degree in economics. Although he held a number of positions after he graduated, none of them had for Scott any real long term appeal. This was discouraging. The only thing that did show up was a consistent (but mostly ignored) tug toward medicine. Scott had decided against a career in medicine when he was an undergrad. With each passing year, this option seemed even less likely. He had watched several of his friends go through medical school and knew the commitment it required. No, it was too late. And yet, the interest kept surfacing. Scott fought this internal tug for years. Until one day he made an important realization.

He pushed the fast forward button on his life, as if he were watching it unfold on video. From the vantage point of the end of his life, he looked back and knew that if he didn't do anything to pursue medicine, he'd regret not knowing what might have happened. He decided he didn't want to live with that. He had to find out. With each step he took, the doors opened.

First, he enrolled in the required courses to apply to medical school. He needed to know if he could earn grades competitive enough to be considered. His first semester confirmed it. He was competitive. Next, he studied for an entire summer for one test, the MCAT, an eight-hour qualifying entrance exam required to apply to medical school. After waiting several weeks to find out how he did, again, he received good news. His scores were competitive. Finally, he began the lengthy process of applying to medical school. This is where it became unpredictable.

Each medical school looks for something different. There is a limit to the number of schools to which you can apply. Scott was advised to play it safe and only apply to schools in which he would have a strong chance. Because Scott had worked for several years before applying to medical school he was considered a "non-traditional" applicant. Some schools were looking for older students. Others weren't interested. He was told not to waste an application on the top tier schools. As much as this conventional wisdom made sense, Scott again decided that he'd regret not knowing what might have happened if he only applied to one of these schools. When the applications were in the mail, a handful had been sent to top medical schools. Then the real work began.

One of the toughest parts of this process was waiting. Getting the mail each day became an important event. An envelope containing our future could show up on any given day. Many days there was nothing. Other days there were invitations to interview. As the weeks and months unfolded, these interviews were followed by a response. Several "no thank you's" came along with a "yes." Relief! Scott knew he was one of the fortunate applicants to receive an offer. And then another offer came. Finally, the day we had to decide if we would move to the mid-west or move to the east coast, our answer came in the mail. We would do neither. A medical school on the west coast invited Scott to join its ranks. He was going to Stanford. We were both ecstatic.

So there we were, packing up our life, excited for the adventure that was about to begin.

Given the craziness of our summer, we had one free weekend in July to make a trip to our new community in hopes of finding a place to live. Stanford, which is located in Palo Alto, is planted right in the middle of the Silicon Valley. At the time of our move, the dot.com craze was at its peak. We had been told that it would be challenging to find a place to live. Coming from southern California, we thought it wouldn't be that much of an adjustment. We had no idea what was in store.

It wasn't just that housing was expensive. We soon discovered that the demand for housing far exceeded the supply. When we arrived in Palo Alto, our first stop was the housing office at Stanford. We learned that it usually took two to three weeks to find a place to live. We had two to three days. We knew we had to act quickly. After making several calls we headed to our first open house.

Typically, when a property was being leased, a one to two hour open house was scheduled. These open house events often felt a lot like a job interview. You had to show up during the stated time. If you were even remotely interested, you were advised to submit an application. There were always several interested parties. The first open house we went to was a two-bedroom apartment. It was old and dark. We weren't very excited about it. We also had complete sticker shock. The monthly rent was the equivalent of what you would pay for a beautiful home in Southern California. Several thousand dollars was required just to move in. We quickly moved on.

Another one we visited had close to 30 people swarming around the place like bees. We overheard one couple talking with the property manager about the Ivy League school they graduated from, where they were working now, and who they knew that he also knew. We heard another person advising a friend to offer to pay more than the stated lease amount. All this strategizing was for a tiny one bedroom apartment! It was insane.

We finally stopped to eat dinner that first evening. Just as we received our food, our mobile phone rang. It was one of the property owners we had called earlier. She told us she had listed the property earlier in the day. Several other people had called before us but we were the first ones she had reached directly. She was willing to meet us. We took our food "to go" and met her at the house ten minutes later.

Unlike other places we looked at, this one had potential. The house was a small cottage, but it had several charming features. We noticed the hardwood floors, the brick fireplace, a cozy office area with built-in bookshelves, an attached garage with laundry hookups, a cheery kitchen, and a yard. It was also only two blocks from Stanford. Being close to campus was one of our most important values. As I walked through this place, I couldn't help but think about a list I had written in my journal a few weeks earlier. I had composed a detailed description of things I wanted in our new home and told God it would be great if we could have them. Essentially, this house had everything on my list. The weird thing was, even though it had everything on my list, it looked different than what I imagined, and I wasn't sure I liked it. Scott had a similar reaction.

One of the biggest drawbacks was the yard. I only call it a yard because it was obviously within the defined boundaries of the property. It was a pretty generous size, but it offered nothing. It hadn't been cared for in years. There was no patio. No grass. No life. Only a broken down fence, lots of weeds and a hard packed cement-like dirt on the ground. It was desolate. I knew it was unusual to find a home with this much outdoor space, and yet, it was so uninviting. This was ironic. I love working outdoors. Gardening is one of my favorite pastimes. But this was too much for me to tackle. I couldn't do it on my own. There was only one possibility that kept us interested.

The owner told us she had just purchased the property and planned to work on the yard. She said she wanted to enhance the looks of the property. This sounded good, but we had no idea if or when it would really happen. We knew we had to make up our minds that evening or it would go to someone else. She was showing it to other people the next day. After seeing another place later that evening in which we had no interest, we made a decision. We took the cottage. So much of it fit the criteria we had hoped to find. If progress wasn't made on the yard, we rationalized, we could always move again.

We were stunned when we moved in a little over a month later. When I pulled into the driveway, I immediately noticed things were different. The old broken down fence was gone. A new, freshly painted, white picket fence soon replaced it. A beautiful aggregate patio had been laid. A sprinkler system was being installed. Very attractive outdoor lighting was strategically placed throughout the yard. Grass was planted. This home was coming to life. An amazing transformation had begun.

Now, two years later, I find it hard to believe it is the same place we initially visited. It's given Scott and me hours of pleasure, both working in and simply enjoying it. It has provided a colorful backdrop for many outdoor gatherings. Just today I got an email from a friend confirming plans to join us next week for dinner. She let me know that she'd been telling her husband about the garden and was so excited he'd finally get to see it.

So what's the point in all of this? How does this relate to having a clear, compelling vision? Sometimes a clear and compelling vision gets its start with nothing more than an occasional internal tug. Sometimes a clear and compelling vision is born out of circumstances that seem as lifeless as a broken down fence and weeds. Sometimes a clear and compelling vision is gaining momentum at a time when nothing could seem further from the truth. As I watch Scott's vision take shape, as I experience my own life path unfold, and as I share in the lives of my friends, family, clients, and colleagues, I keep returning to several important life lessons. These guiding principles nurture a clear, compelling vision and offer support in living an intentional life.

Start Where You Are

This summer, Scott and I spent a week in Illinois visiting relatives and attending a huge family reunion. While we were there, one of Scott's cousins gave us a book she thought we would enjoy reading. We loved it. Each of us sped through it in hours. The book, *It's Not About the Bike: My Journey Back to Life*, is Lance Armstrong's story of his incredible fight against cancer, his road to recovery, and his eventual domination of the world of competitive cycling. At the time we read his book this summer, he had just won his fourth straight Tour De France victory. Before reading the book, I knew the Tour De France took place each year, but I had no idea of the intensity of the physical and mental challenge it involved.

The Tour De France is arguably the most grueling athletic competition on the planet. The race is a 21-day competition, taking 200 cyclists on a 2,290 mile trek around the entire circumference of France. The terrain is fraught with every sort of challenge imaginable. Some days the blazing sun is so intense, the road appears to melt before their eyes. Other days involve steep ascents up the Pyrenees mountains, a climb accompanied with bone chilling rain, sleet and dense fog that can take out even the world's best riders. The cyclists ride closely together in a pack called the peloton. Racing at high speeds, there is always the danger that one false move in the peloton will create a domino effect collision. One race day under these conditions is enough to tap the reserves of any competitive athlete. To compete for 21 days requires an endurance that can only be achieved through disciplined, rigorous training.

In his book, Lance Armstrong tells how he was diagnosed with testicular cancer at age 25. His odds to live through it were less than 40%. (He found out later his odds were actually much lower than the 40% his doctors initially told him.) His competitive spirit shifted immediately from cycling to cancer. Now he was fighting for his life. Two surgeries later and several months into his treatment, he realized just how much the cancer had weakened him. He liked to keep riding his bike between chemo treatments. It told him and others, if he could still ride, he must be doing okay. One day he went for a ride in his neighborhood with a few friends. He thought he was doing a good job of keeping up with them. What he didn't realize was how slowly his friends were riding just so he could keep up. At one point they rode up a short, steep hill. As he was struggling to keep peddling, a woman in her 50's rode by him effortlessly on a heavy mountain bike. He was not the world class competitor he had once been. But he didn't stop riding. While he continued to fight for his life, he continued to get on his bike.

In time, he was given a clean bill of health. He had won the war against cancer. Through a series of stops and starts, he eventually found his way back to competitive cycling. Some people had written him off. They didn't think he'd ever be a serious contender again. They were wrong. Three years after he was initially diagnosed with cancer, he won the Tour De France.

What is the message here? Wherever you are in your journey, you are right on track. You may be having a Tour De France victory year. Or you may be reeling from unexpected circumstances that present a tremendous setback. You may be in a season of getting back on your feet and gaining momentum. Wherever you are, you are not a day late or a day ahead of schedule.

You don't have to have your act together. You don't have to have things figured out. You don't have to be performing at a "world class" level. If you desire to live with a clear and compelling vision, the best place to start is where you are. This doesn't mean you have to like where you are, it just means you let it be what it is. Don't strive or fight it. Embrace it and trust that all of the events in your life, the good and the bad, have a hand in shaping your vision.

Start a LIFE Portfolio

Reading Lance Armstrong's story stirred up reminders of my own struggle several years ago. While I wasn't in a physically life threatening situation, in many ways, I felt like my life was dying. I raced through my 20's enjoying my work and my life, but a growing dissatisfaction and uncertainty began to emerge. Even though I was well-established in an exciting career, I found myself feeling plateaud, stagnant, and pretty thin on fresh dreams for my life. This was scary.

I had always had definite ideas about what I was doing and where I would go next. I valued living a purposeful life. But at this point, everything started falling apart. For the first time I could remember, I didn't have any dreams for my life. My life looked very similar to our broken down fence and weedy yard in Palo Alto the first time we saw it. It had few signs of life.

At some point during this difficult transition, my employer offered a two-day "life planning" seminar. I had no idea the impact those two days would have on my life. For starters, I had time and space to think about my life with no limits, no judgment, and no holding back. I also got a lot of perspective.

One of the things that impacted me the most was a study on students at Yale. The study revealed that only 3% of the students in the study had identified and written life and career goals when they graduated. Twenty years later, the satisfaction, quality of life, and financial wealth of the 3% far exceeded that of the other 97%! Whether you are a "goal" person or you get there another way, the 3 % approach is all about living your life with intention. Living life in the 3 % was what I wanted.

I started where I was and kept it pretty simple. I got a notebook and wrote down two desires. I wanted fresh dreams for my life. I didn't have any in mind at the time, so I thought this was a good place to start. I also wanted to get rid of some debt I had. Given how stuck I was at the time, I thought meeting with a professional counselor would be a helpful way to work through this and come up with some new dreams. I didn't have the extra money for this, but I wrote down my list and trusted God would come through. What happened next was very creative.

Not too long after I wrote my list, my car was stolen in the middle of the day out of a fairly small parking lot outside my office complex. People I worked with had been moving furniture in and out of the parking lot area throughout the day. It seemed so unlikely. How could my car be stolen with so many people around who knew it was mine?

I filed reports with the police and my insurance company. The policy was to wait 30 days to see if my car was found. If not, the insurance company would settle. Days turned into weeks and nothing happened. The car was not recovered. I was convinced it had been driven into Mexico. This was easy to do from where I lived in southern California, just two hours north of the border.

Finally, the 30 days passed and the insurance company settled. They gave me the top value for my car, probably more than I could have sold it for myself. Then just a couple days after we settled, the car was found. It was only a few miles away at a nearby movie theater. Had that happened two days earlier, I would have been stuck with the car, which had been pretty beat up since it was stolen.

Instead, I had an insurance settlement. The money enabled me to eliminate debt, cut my car expenses in half, and begin meeting with a professional counselor to help sort through where I was and where I wanted to go next. Amazing.

In time, I did begin to get fresh dreams for my life. As they showed up, I captured them in my notebook. A year went by, then two, then three. As time passed, it was exciting to watch a seed of an idea grow into reality in my life. One of these seeds got its start with some thoughts I wrote down in 1994. I had been thinking about graduate school and also wanted to know more about work as an interpersonal communication consultant. I found myself writing questions like, "Does this job exist? What training and education is required? Where could I find out more?"

The road ahead wasn't clear cut. I did go back to graduate school and got a degree in communication management. Most of the positions I found out about in school however, weren't what I was interested in doing. Not until after I graduated did I discover and start working with a communication consulting firm in Los Angeles. It was like finding the needle in the haystack.

Three years had passed when I re-read what I originally wrote in my life book. I was now doing the very thing I had wondered about several years earlier.

I'm now in my second decade of keeping a life notebook. Not all the ideas I write down come into being. This is a good thing. We grow and change and so do our desires. This is what's great about writing things down. One of the most powerful benefits of keeping a written account of my life is that I get answers! My life speaks back to me from paper. I don't have to look hard to see what's truly important. The themes and patterns over time are undeniable.

Losing sight of what is true is easy, especially during a difficult season in life. If you want a clear, compelling vision for your life, capture on paper your dreams, hopes, inspirations, and ideas along the way. You won't have to find your vision. Your vision will find you.

Think of it as if you were managing a stock portfolio. If you wanted to see how your stocks were doing today, what would you do to find out where you stand? My guess is you would check your online account or pull out a recent statement. Both of these make it easy to track and evaluate the performance of financial investments. What if I were to ask you about how your life investments are doing? Would you have a similar portfolio to look at? Many people I've encountered are looking for direction in their life, but they've invested very little in the process. Invest more in your life by starting your own life portfolio. Here are several ideas to help you get started:

1. **Satisfaction Audit:** Write down whatever comes to mind in response to the following three statements: "What I like about my life right now. What I don't like about my life right now. How I would like my life to look different six months from now."

2. **Do/Have/Help/Become:** Take inventory of the things you'd like to do, the things you'd like to have, the people you'd like to help, and the person you want to become. Give each item target dates to help prioritize your time, energy, and resources.

3. **Sunday Night Litmus Test:** This is one of my favorites. Ask yourself, "What would my life look like if I could go to bed Sunday night eager and excited for Monday and the week to begin?" Be specific.

4. **The Clean Slate:** Here's a similar idea with a broader focus. Daydream that you wake up tomorrow morning and the slate is wiped clean. That means...no connection to the past. No attachments to people, projects, budgets, income, family, roles, responsibilities...you get the picture? Now, design your life. What do you create? Who are you? How do people see you? What is your passion? What is your legacy?

Write whatever comes to mind. No limits, no holding back, just let yourself go. (If this feels uncomfortable, remember it's just an exercise, you can have your life back when you're done.)

5. **Things I Love:** Enough said. Jot down everything you enjoy doing and being. Anything in which you are interested, excited, brings you pleasure, or fills your emotional bank account goes here.

Start With Support

Yesterday I did something I've never done before. I ran 12 miles. I'm only doing it now because of a marathon I'm running in later this year. The idea to run in this marathon came from a woman in my Catalyst group, a support and accountability group started by my friend Sue. Julianne shared with us about the marathon for which she was training. I was so impressed. A seed was planted in me and it wouldn't go away. It grew to the point that I was compelled to do something about it.

I knew I couldn't do this on my own. I didn't know the first thing about running in a marathon. I started researching and found a marathon with a training program. This program gives me the structure I desperately need to achieve my goal. I meet with my training group each month. Every two weeks I get a new training schedule to follow. I have a dedicated coach with whom I'm in constant email contact. I'm ten weeks into the training and on track. And I'm doing things I would never do on my own.

A weight loss research study I read recently reported similar results. The study found that individuals whose weight loss programs included regularly meeting with a group lost three times the weight as those who were attempting to do it on their own.

A few weeks ago I got a voice mail message from several women who were in a WIN (Women's Intention Network) coaching group I started. Their message was so exciting. They were together at a restaurant in the middle of a big party. The party was a celebration for one of the women who had just finished graduate school. It was a major accomplishment. It was also one of many milestones that has been shared and celebrated among this group of women. The amazing thing is, the group hasn't met formally now for more than two years. The powerful support, encouragement, and synergy that started when the group first met together continues to inspire us all on our individual paths.

Tomorrow I have a phone appointment with one of my closest friends. This call that I look forward to each week is one of the best things that came out of the life planning seminar I went to years ago. At that time, several friends started what we called the 3% Club. We wanted to live deliberate lives like the students in the Yale study. We began meeting together regularly to help encourage each other's dreams and vision. To this day, ten years later, my friend Nancy and I still have weekly 3% appointments to plan, share, and support each other in our journeys. In phone or in person, these lifelines encourage us on our path.

One of the reasons 12 Step programs are so successful is that participants acknowledge they don't have the power to change on their own. They admit a need for a higher power.

Am I making my point? We live in a relational world. If you want a clear, compelling vision, you need the support of others. Find an intention partner. Start your own 3% club. Hire a coach. Surround yourself with people who respect you and inspire you to live out your true purpose.

Over the years, each new person I've encountered has taught me an important lesson. No two of us are alike. We are each unique, one-of-a-kind creations. This changes the definition of a successful life. What does it mean to live life well? Life at its best is when we are being ourselves.

If you want your own clear and compelling vision:

Start where you are: Allow all of the events of your life, the good and the bad, to have a hand in shaping your vision.

Start a life portfolio: Find a special notebook and fill it with your hopes, dreams, desires, intentions, values, and purposes. Check in with it often and watch your path unfold.

Start with support: Partner with someone else and encourage each other on your paths.

You are an original. There is no one else like you. Your story isn't finished yet. So get started. Begin the great adventure and let your vision find you.

About
Sharon Nichols

Sharon Nichols works with mid-career professionals to ignite their true purpose in their work, in their lives, and in their communication. She is particularly focused on helping "30-40 somethings" navigate change, re-define values and priorities, and create a fresh focus and renewed enthusiasm for the next chapter of their lives.

Sharon's calm and welcoming presence puts people at ease. Non-judgmental, unhurried, and attentive, Sharon is a skilled thought partner, listening ear, devoted supporter, and sounding board. She offers the truth, shares perspective and insight, but her style is more about asking than telling. She helps individuals discover the answers, resources, and wisdom they already have inside.

Before starting her own coaching practice, Sharon was a consultant with a communication management firm in Los Angeles. She served as a coach and advisor to mid- and senior-level corporate clients focused on enhancing personal credibility, communication effectiveness, and leadership. Corporate clients she has worked with include Dell, Amgen, ARCO, Palm, The Los Angeles Times and others. Prior to consulting, Sharon implemented numerous training and leadership development initiatives for employees of a non-profit ministry organization.

Sharon is a member of the International Coach Federation, Fast Company's Silicon Valley Company of Friends, and the Bay Area Association of Psychological Type.

She is a certified facilitator of The Coaching Clinic™ and is qualified to interpret the Myers-Briggs Type Indicator.

Sharon is also on the staff of Stanford University's Graduate School of Business where she is an instructor and communication coach with the Management Communication Program.

She earned an M.A. in Communication Management from the Annenberg School for Communication at the University of Southern California and received her B.S. in Behavioral Sciences from California State Polytechnic University, Pomona.

Sharon and her husband Scott live in Palo Alto, CA where they enjoy reading, travel, exploring the many great Bay Area restaurants, slowing down in their garden, an occasional tandem bike ride, and being a part of The River Church Community in San Jose.

For additional resources, visit Sharon's website at www.intentioncoaching.com, call (650) 251-9413, or email her at sharon@intentioncoaching.com.

Inner Pathways to Vision
Five Ways to Move Beyond Your Barriers

By Claudette Rowley

"Your vision will become clear only when you can look into your heart. Who looks outside, dreams. Who looks inside, awakens."
~ Carl Jung

Sitting down to compose this chapter, I am intimately aware of my own desire to design and implement a compelling vision for a new chapter of my own life. I am expecting my first child in several weeks. Talk about creating a new vision! I am grateful to be in touch with my ability to select and manifest a vision for my family, my work, and myself that elevates my life to an exciting and satisfying level.

I remember a time when my ability to choose a compelling vision wasn't clear to me. I was never sure exactly what I wanted. Even if I did know what I desired, I didn't believe that I could achieve it or that I even deserved to have it. Was I wrong! The opportunity to identify a vision, build it, and see it actualized in the world is available to each person on the planet. It's part of fulfilling your potential as a human being.

I'd like to share with you what I've experienced, learned, and observed about creating a compelling vision. This chapter will examine the process of moving your vision from the internal (the picture you see with your mind's eye) to the external (the implementation of your vision). Specifically, the chapter will explore:

- How to identify a vision that's compelling for you.
- What blocks a clear view of your vision.
- How to build your vision.
- Knowing when to expand your vision and when to move on.

What is a Compelling Vision?

I define a compelling vision as the act of pushing past your internal barriers to embrace what you deeply and fundamentally desire in any area of your life—work, relationships, health, spirituality, or fun. Included in the process of creating a compelling vision is giving yourself full permission to identify what you would LOVE to manifest in your life. *You get to want what you want.*

For many of us, limitations in thoughts and beliefs about what is possible create internal barriers to recognizing our vision. Growing up, we interpret our experiences and the messages we receive through socialization to develop a set of beliefs that we live by. Since many beliefs that we've constructed are based on past experiences, they may limit us in the present moment. For example, a pertinent belief at age ten will most likely be limiting to you at age thirty. At one time or another, we all make up rules about what we are allowed to have or want or desire.

Since vision is based on knowing what you truly desire, it's helpful to examine the thoughts and beliefs that hold you back from what you want. Freeing yourself from internal barriers releases you to identify, build, and actualize a vision based on your deepest desires and wildest dreams. One of the keys to selecting and implementing a vision—knowing what's right for you—is listening closely to your inner voice.

My Inner What?

Your inner voice is another name for your unique, internal wisdom—the part of yourself that knows what is true and best for you. Although we are each born with this wisdom intact, it often gets swallowed in a sea of external voices, opinions, and judgments.

Learning to hear your inner voice strengthens your ability to identify your compelling vision. Your access to this wisdom assists you in knowing if you are selecting the biggest, most fulfilling vision for you. You inner voice guides you as you build your vision and gives you direction as you decide whether to expand or release a vision. Here are five of the pathways to accessing your inner voice.

Five Pathways to Listening to Your Inner Voice

1. Tap Into Your Heart's Wisdom

Social conditioning teaches us to be logical and "use our heads." When you only use your head, your experience of yourself and the world is limited. You miss out on vital information from your emotions.

Benefits: The same neurological tissue found in the brain is found in the heart. The heart is a second "brain" and our emotional center. Listening to your head and your heart is crucial to good decision-making about your life, business, relationships, and vision.

New Focus: Put your hand over your heart and focus there. What is your heart's message?

2. Connect With Your Body

Your body gives you a tremendous amount of useful information that you may not be conscious of. For example, when your mother-in-law visits, does your stomach tie up in knots? When your boss yells at you, do your shoulders turn into stone? When you feel passionate and alive, does your chest feel warm and open? When we ignore the body's message, we lose valuable information designed to let us know what works for us and what doesn't.

Benefits: For many people, fear manifests as tightness in their chest. This is valuable information, especially if you aren't aware that you are afraid. Your body alerts you to what makes you feel passionate and what doesn't. The body is a fount of wisdom designed to tell you when you're on the right path and when you aren't.

New Focus: Notice the messages your body is giving you right now. Try a self-massage to find areas in your back, neck, or shoulders that are tense or knotted. What other areas of your body feel tight? Which ones feel relaxed and loose? Use this information as another pathway to listening to your inner wisdom.

3. Listen to Your Intuition

Intuition is simply knowing something, without knowing how you know it. Connect back to a time that you had a "gut feeling" about something. Perhaps you were offered a job you knew you shouldn't take, even though it looked good on the surface, or you were in a relationship that just felt right for you. That's your intuition talking.

Benefits: Intuition presents you with a wealth of information. Remember that your intuition is never wrong, although your interpretation of it may be incorrect. When your intuition calls to you, trust it. Practice makes perfect when it comes to effectively using this sense of knowing.

New Focus: The next time you need to make a decision, check in with your intuition. Experiment with trusting it. When you follow your intuition, what happens? When you hear it and disregard it, what's the outcome?

4. Notice Your Self-Saboteur

Each of us has our very own special saboteur. The saboteur is the voice in your head that says, "You are not good enough." "Who do you think you are?" "If you take this new job, everyone will find out what a fraud you are." The saboteur mistakenly believes that it is protecting you when it stops you from making changes or taking a risk.

Benefits: Learn to distinguish between your voice and the saboteur's messages. Be aware of the saboteur's ability to drive your choices and decisions.

New Focus: Simply notice the negative voices playing in your head. Notice the times when they crop up. Recognize that the voices aren't you and they aren't true. When you learn to separate your inner voice from that of the saboteur, you begin to change your life.

5. Identify Limiting Beliefs

We each carry a set of beliefs that we live by. Certain beliefs you hold consciously, while others are mainly unconscious. Beliefs develop out of past experiences and our interpretations of those experiences. Some of the conscious and unconscious beliefs that you develop limit your ability to grow and move forward in your life. For example: One of your goals as a successful entrepreneur is to make a lot of money. You discover that you have a belief—a limiting one—that it's wrong to make a lot of money. Until you begin to alter your beliefs about money, it will be more difficult for you to achieve that financial success you desire.

Benefits: Learning to notice a limiting belief allows you to become conscious of it, and then change it. Releasing a belief that limits you puts you back in the driver's seat of your life. You, rather than an old belief, make the choices that are right for you and allow you to fulfill your potential.

Ways to spot a limiting belief:

1. You tell yourself that you only have one or two choices in a situation or "no choice" at all.
2. Your saboteur expresses its opinion, generally based on a limiting belief.
3. A decision may appear to be black and white to you, or an either/or situation.
4. You have decided that "this is the way the world is."
5. You make a decision based on fear.
6. You feel constricted and notice that you lack clarity about a specific situation.

New Focus: How does a particular belief allow you to attract what you really want in life? How does it prevent you from identifying your vision and attaining your goals? When you reach an obstacle in your path, make sure that it's not an old belief in your way.

You Get to Want What You Want

"WHAT'S TERRIBLE IS TO PRETEND THAT THE SECOND-RATE IS FIRST-RATE. TO PRETEND THAT YOU DON'T NEED LOVE WHEN YOU DO; OR YOU LIKE YOUR WORK WHEN YOU KNOW QUITE WELL YOU'RE CAPABLE OF BETTER." ~ DORIS LESSING

When you tap into your inner voice and identify your vision, you bring to life your deepest longing. Your vision manifests the essence of you based on your truth, values, creativity, and authenticity. Putting yourself out into the world in this way can feel risky; the thought of that risk can easily block you from seeing your vision.

A vision can be small or large, and have an impact on your daily life or the big picture of your life. For example, a vision of the ideal day care situation for my baby forms in my mind as his birth grows closer. I'm counting on the vision of what I truly desire to assist in attracting the optimal child care situation. In the whole scheme of life, this is a smaller vision, yet no less important. And this "smaller" vision makes a direct impact on my ability to realize my far-reaching vision for my coaching business.

A vision that's compelling for you is often right at your fingertips. We all have an inkling of the vision we'd like to put into the world: the forgotten dream, the "ridiculous" idea, and the "unrealistic" business venture. You are born knowing what you want at your deepest core. After awhile, many of us begin to settle for what we think we're allowed to have. "Just okay" becomes good enough. "It's fine" becomes a way of life. The parameters of our wanting become defined by what the saboteur and family, friends, or a significant other tell us we are allowed to have.

I was recently speaking with a client about this exact topic. Patrick related to me that at some point in his life, he just stopped dreaming. Caught up in the routine of daily life, he stopped thinking about his visions for the present and the future. At the end of our coaching session, I gave Patrick an exercise to take away and ponder. His task was to look at eight areas of his life: health, career, money, friends and family, fun and recreation, physical environment, and personal growth, and create a vision that he'd LOVE to be living for each one. During our next call, he revealed his visions to me. We discovered that he had equated vision with what he was willing to live with. I pushed him to tap into what he would really love to manifest in his life. **You Get To Want What You Want.** This is where vision is born.

Believe it or not, there is no "judge of desire" holding court to decide if your vision is legitimate or not. "Well, Bill's been a good boy and his want is modest, so he can pursue the career he's always wanted. The vision committee will allow his dream to come true. But Samantha—the committee doesn't believe that her business idea is a go. Too ambitious. Too risky. Who does she think she is?"

Excavating your vision is an act of not only moving past internal barriers, but of claiming the authentic desires that are rightfully yours. In the process, you reclaim yourself.

Signs That You Are On The Right Path

1. Your intuition. You have an intuitive sense or gut feeling that confirms your path.
2. Your energy. Your vision is an energy-booster, not an energy-drainer.
3. Hearing "That's stupid." As odd as it may seen, hearing yourself say or think "That's stupid" or "That's crazy" are both solid indicators that you are on the right track. When you get close to knowing what you want or—gasp—manifesting it, your saboteur will pull out the stops and tell you that it's dumb.
4. Your body. When you think about your vision, how does your body feel? One client gave a great example of her body's wisdom. When she feels passion, she

experiences a frenetic energy from her heart to her nose. In her mind's eye, she sees the energy as silver and spinning like a windmill.

You have full access to your inner wisdom. Check in with your inner voice. What information do you receive? What pathways or clues to your inner voice are uniquely yours?

Vision-Stoppers

"As you grow into your dream, your fears grow along with you. Courage is action in the face of fear."

~ Mary Manin Morrissey

What's the number one vision-stopper?

FEAR. That big, hairy goblin that constricts your breath, tightens shoulders, narrows your world down to the size of a pin hole, and makes you want to jump back in bed and throw the covers back over your head because "What's the use, after all?".

I've observed that the top two manifestations of fear related to vision are:

1. Fear of failure manifested as:
   - Fear that I won't pick the "right" vision.
   - Fear of failure when I attempt to build the vision.
2. Fear of success showing up as:
   - I can't have this great vision. I don't deserve it.
   - Once I have a vision, I must follow through.
   - If I'm actually successful, my identity and life will change into something I don't want.

Another name for the fears of failure and success is RISK. Identify a vision, build it, implement it, and maybe even expand it?! Yikes. As we've discussed, the truest vision for you is the one based on your authentic desires. As a result, putting your vision out into the world can feel like vulnerably placing yourself on display.

The saboteur and any limiting beliefs you hold generate these fears of failure and success. Unchecked, they will stop you in your tracks. You will make an abrupt about face and go back from whence you came.

It's true: fear has an ingenious way of dropping seemingly insurmountable obstacles in your path. Some obstacles result from external circumstances. For example, you are turned down for a job you really wanted or the business plan you hoped would get funded, didn't. Just as many, if not more, obstacles are internally generated by the saboteur. The saboteur loves to cut you off from your inner voice and deny you full access to your intuition, your ability to fully want, and to be at choice. It relishes telling you all sorts of nasty stories about how your vision will fail if you actualize it and how it's too risky to go after your life's passion. The saboteur will play on your limiting beliefs about what's possible for you.

While writing this section, the following vision of fear came to me. You are standing on one side of a river and your beautiful vision lies in wait on the other side. A wooden bridge spans the river. And FEAR has ignited a blazing bonfire of self-doubt and judgment smack in the middle of the bridge, leaving you no easy way to cross. How do you put out the blaze? Do you forget about fear's machinations altogether and swim across the river to the vision that you know is yours?

Mobilizing Fear to Your Advantage

Whether fear is based on past experiences, present concerns, or future worries, fear is simply an emotion. It is not truth about the validity of your experience or of your vision. Here's a visual: your saboteur sits on a treasure chest filled with your rich visions, human potential, and every gift you possess. In other words, the presence of a saboteur indicates treasure to be claimed.

Understanding your saboteur's strategy will assist you in overcoming the mental or emotional obstacles that fear may create for you. Hooking into your intuition, tapping your heart's wisdom, and listening to the wisdom of your body are powerful fear-busters. During my coaching training, I often found myself in a fearful state—fear of the unknown, fear of failure. One of my trainers shared the following powerful perspective that shifted my outlook on fear. Physiologically, fear and excitement manifest the same way in the body. Put another way: where there's fear, there's excitement. That's the nature of risk-taking.

Vision Building

> "A POWERFUL CREATOR PUTS MORE ENERGY AND TRUST INTO THEIR INTERNAL CREATION THAN THEY DO IN THE EXTERNAL CIRCUMSTANCES OF THEIR LIFE." ~ EVA LOVE

Now that you've identified a new compelling vision for yourself or reconnected with an old one, it's time to build it. What will it take for your vision to become a reality?

Warning #1: If you are feeling no fear, do not read this warning! I don't want to generate fear where none exists. If the thought of actualizing your vision makes it difficult to breathe, continue reading. Whether you've felt fear or not up to this point, putting the building blocks of your vision into place is an opportune time for your saboteur and its negative talk to surface. Your saboteur may have been content to let you dabble in visioning, but to actually set goals and plan is a whole different game.

Building Blocks

So far, creating a compelling vision and understanding your own internal obstacles has been largely an internal process. Building your vision combines internal focus with external action.

- Goal-setting. If vision is the house, goals are the foundation and load-bearing walls. Goals move vision forward into concrete existence.
- Strategy. How are you going to get where you want to go?

- Planning. A plan combines strategy with goal setting.
- Support and guidance. You can't do this alone. Successful visions are rarely built alone. Look at anyone who has manifested his or her vision, and you will see a truckload of people who helped them get where they wanted to go. The key here is to ASK for what you want and need. *If you don't ask, the answer is always no.*
- Staying in touch with the big picture—your beautiful vision. Be aware of your powerful ability to create. You are fully at choice and empowered to create each aspect of your life exactly the way you want it to be.
- Connecting with your inner voice as your guide through the process. The five pathways to accessing your inner voice will assist you to stay in your power and out of debilitating fear. Listening to your inner voice will also temper outside influences and opinions. You know what's right for you.

Serena, head of the sales division for a cookware company, described her vision and its supporting goals this way. "My vision is that within five years, my company will be #1 in sales for this cookware niche. We will be bringing in $2 million annually in sales, and have a national and international presence." In order to build her vision, Serena set these goals: cultivate national and international distributors to sell her product in their areas, get large retail chains to carry the cookware line, and to follow up aggressively with former and potential customers.

Warning #2: In the process of manifesting your vision, it can be easy for the "settling demon" to take hold. "Well, as long as I get part of my vision, that's good enough." You get to have every single aspect of your vision realized if that's what you want. Wanting is judgment free. Hold fast to your vision. You deserve to see it come to life. The world needs what you have to offer.

Vision Expansion vs. Release

Once you've realized your vision, then what? Some visions are meant to be expanded beyond the original. Some aren't. In certain cases, the vision may continue to exist while its creator moves on. These decisions are a function of your style and desire. Most visions require expansion to continue to thrive, just as human beings require continued growth and evolution to find success and satisfaction in life.

Common Vision Traps

- You feel chained to your vision forever. "Now that I've built my vision, I must stay with it. Even if I don't want to."
- You have blinders on. You miss recognizing the expansion necessary to keep your vision alive and ensure its success. "My initial vision is actualized—okay, I'm done."
- You don't honor your own vision style. Some people are vision-expanders and some are vision-starters. Vision-expanders build their vision and continue to grow it and move it forward. For vision-starters, the joy is in the initial design and implementation of the vision. Once their idea comes to life, these folks get bored and restless, ready to move on to the next idea. Both styles are valid.

Messages From Your Inner Voice

Boredom, restlessness, or frustration can be clues that a vision needs to be tweaked, expanded, or let go. I often encounter people who criticize themselves for not wanting to follow through with a vision to the end, or who judge themselves for getting bored and restless with a vision. One client summed up her style well when she said, "I'm a great opener and closer." Each time she built a vision successfully, she grew bored and dissatisfied. Eventually, she realized that her strength lay in the initial implementation of the vision.

Once it was up and running, she was ready to move on to the next vision.

Other clients report that restlessness or boredom can signal the need to expand their vision to the next level of development. They may grow dissatisfied with the current incarnation of a vision, while still loving the vision itself. While it's natural for restlessness, frustration, or boredom to crop up temporarily, if you encounter these emotions repeatedly, they may be a message from your inner voice that this vision no longer works for you in its present state.

When the question "What's next?" begins running through your mind repeatedly, take notice. It's a message from your intuition telling you to look at the situation and be clear about what you want.

Vision Expansion

You've decided that its time to expand your vision. What's the best way for expansion to take place? Simply follow the same steps you took to build your initial vision. Be clear about what you truly want. Identify any fears blocking your vision. Check in with your inner voice for clarity about your path. Set your goals and start to build the next exciting phase of your vision!

What Are Your Undreamed Dreams?

When the Berlin Wall fell and Germany was reunified, the German people experienced the fulfillment of an undreamed dream. The destruction of the wall seemed out of their hands, and they hadn't let themselves even consider the possibility of reunification. Dreams like that could only lead to disappointment. When their undreamed dream came true, the Germans were unprepared and caught off guard. How sad to stop dreaming about what you most want for fear of not getting it.

What are your undreamed dreams? What visions brew inside of you that you don't entertain for fear of disappointment? What risk do you need to take?

What's the Life You Would LOVE to Live Right Now?

Remember that when you ask for what you want, the answer has a greater chance of being YES. By embracing your dreams and visions, you are almost assured a life of aliveness and passion. The world craves your vision. If we each manifested our human potential through big, beautiful, authentic visions, think how different the world would be.

About
Claudette Rowley

Claudette Rowley, MSW, CPCC (Certified Professional Co-Active Coach) has been actively engaged in the development of human potential since 1991 through her work in consulting, program development, writing and coaching. She founded her coaching firm, MetaVoice, in early 2000 and has coached fulltime ever since. The foundation of Claudette's work is the belief that each of us possesses the potential for great magnificence. The key to uncovering our magnificence is the ability to connect to authentic self. Authentic self is found when we have the courage to live according to our own rules and give expression to a life that meshes with who we fundamentally are. Claudette's vision is to raise the level of human consciousness in the world through her coaching and writing.

Claudette loves coaching entrepreneurs and leaders who want to harness their full potential and soar to new heights as human beings. She is attracted to clients who want to push their own edges to create successful start up businesses, overcome self-sabotage, understand their impact as leaders and enjoy the rewards of risk taking. She believes that it is the internal focus of believing in yourself, listening to your intuition, and tuning into your emotions that allows her clients to realize visions that far exceed their dreams.

Claudette is known for her intuitive style, her ability to get to the heart of a matter, and her passion for challenging people to move out of their comfort zones. She holds a BA and MSW from the University of Michigan, and received her coaching certification from the Coaches Training Institute.

To her work, she brings a fresh eye and a passion for her clients' personal and professional success.

Claudette writes and produces a monthly newsletter "Insights for Savvy Entrepreneurs" for aspiring and seasoned entrepreneurs (and anyone else who wants a monthly shot of inspiration). To contact Claudette or subscribe to her newsletter, visit www.metavoice.org, e-mail her at info@metavoice.org or call (781) 676-5633. She looks forward to hearing from you!

Living Your Vision® ~ From the Inside Out

By Fran Fisher

"YOUR VISION WILL BECOME CLEAR, ONLY WHEN YOU LOOK INTO YOUR HEART. WHO LOOKS OUTSIDE DREAMS. WHO LOOKS INSIDE AWAKENS."
~ CARL JUNG

Living Your Vision… Reflect on this idea for a moment... What thoughts or images come to your mind?

What I see is this: our beautiful planet suspended in space and all the human beings on the earth are living rich and fulfilling lives, each one *living* their personal vision.

This vision compels me to ask for spiritual guidance daily, to listen for the direction, and follow through with passion and courage. I hold this vision as a possibility. I believe this is a vision of the Garden of Eden—an allegory depicting the Divine Intention for our human experience. This is the true reality of the universe, the natural state, and anything other than that is an illusion I hold of my separation from that reality.

Imagine for a moment how life would be different if *everyone* was fully, authentically self-expressed, living their life aligned and congruent with his or her unique and Divinely guided vision, purpose, and values.

How would *your* life be different if you were fully manifesting your personal vision, purpose, and values in every aspect of your life: personal well-being, family, intimate relationships, career, money, etc.? What is different for me is more freedom, more creativity, less fear, more self-acceptance, more joy, more prosperity, and more *love*.

At a cocktail party a couple of years ago, someone walked up to me and asked, "What do *you* do for a living?" I could honestly say, without hesitation, "I *be* me all day long and I get paid abundantly for it!"

What I *do* empowers me to *be* my authentic Self. These aspects of being and doing have converged in my life: *Who I am* is *what I do.*

I used to feel like I was leading two separate lives. One was my inner life of spirituality and sense of mission to make a difference. That felt like the real me, passionate and deeply loving. The other life, my outer life, overshadowed the inner life like a bulldozer. This was my day-to-day life where I was driven to succeed in the world and to survive financially. The tension between the two was confusing, frustrating, and unsatisfying—almost unbearable. To relieve the pressure, I sought answers—mostly outside of myself (psychics, counselors, self-help books and tapes, and transformational workshops galore).

In spite of all that I learned from those sources, my journey took me deeper into darkness. The year 1980 was a dark-night-of-the-soul year for me. I was a single parent raising two pre-teenagers. I was struggling with lack of money and in breakdown on my career path. A long-term relationship with a man had just ended, my son had gone to live with his father 1,200 miles away, and I had just been diagnosed with a debilitating disease.

In March of 1981, I was invited to attend a "firewalk" experience. I was assured that for $50 and only one evening of my life, I would experience once-and-for-all that fear is an illusion and it doesn't have to stop me from doing anything I truly believe in.

The fact that I *did* have the courage to walk on coals that are hot enough to melt aluminum and that I *didn't* burn my feet *did* bust up my belief that fear was real. That alone was a priceless gift I gave myself. I learned something else that night that became one of the cornerstones of the transformational Living Your Vision® process—a process that I developed ten years later.

I learned there are four steps to achieving *anything:*

1. Discover: Who am I?
2. Clarify: What do I want?
3. Create: Design a plan to achieve it.
4. Act: Work the plan.

I applied that formula for a decade. I cleared up the disease, and I manifested a new intimate relationship, a dream job, a prestigious position and salary, and career growth—and I nearly ruined my health *again* in the process.

In 1990 my life-long pattern of work-a-holism finally caught up with me. I was *such a mess* from working 18-hour days over six days a week for two years straight! I couldn't hold a teacup in my hand for fear of dropping and breaking it. I called an intervention on myself by flying across the country to the Oregon coast and walking the beach for a week.

What I heard in the stillness, with the comforting sound of the ocean waves in the background, was this: "Fran, it is time to put *yourself* in the center of your life." Everything became clear to me in that moment. I had nearly killed myself trying to fix and resolve and manage and control the circumstances, constantly in a reactive mode. I was making things happen, oh, yes *indeed*, but I was operating my life from the outside in instead of from the inside out.

I had defined my "Who am I?" based on what I was *doing*, not on who I was *being*. I didn't *really* know who I was inside. And, I had been afraid to look.

I took a courageous year off for healing the addiction—to learn how to put myself in the center—to learn to love myself enough to make choices that brought *me* fulfillment and pleasure—to discover my values and learn to honor them. The year was by far the most painful of my life. The work-a-holism had been a place to hide out so that I didn't have to be with me. I planned the year so that I didn't have anything I *absolutely had* to do. That left me with quiet time to be with myself. And I found that looking at who I had become was more painful than grieving my mother's death.

Charlene

Then Charlene appeared in my life. She was a hypnotherapist and a "closet" psychic, afraid to let people know of her gift of clairvoyance. She was struggling to pay her rent, working at a part-time job where she wasn't happy, and deeply desiring to live her passion and share her gifts. She asked me to help her. My intuition felt the "yes," even as it was coming out of my mouth.

Not having a clue, consciously, what I was doing, I asked Charlene a few questions about herself and her values and what she held as meaningful.

I didn't ask her questions about her career desires or marketing goals. The starting place was to discover her core essence, the unalterable truth of her being, regardless of the outer circumstances. What I know about entrepreneurs from my own experience is that they think who they are is their business. They have it backwards. Who they are is *so* much greater and grander than what they do for a living. Who they *are* is what they take to their business and their relationships and to every other aspect of their life. Their business is an *expression* of who they are.

If we had started creating her success plan by creating a compelling vision of her business or her life, it would have been an outside-of-herself vision—a vision of a future state that she would aspire to get to someday. Rather than trying to get *to* something, I wanted to assist Charlene in accessing the essence of who she already *is*. This would be the empowering self-awareness or personal power that she would take to all the circumstances in her life.

Nothing in the manifest universe exists, but that it is born first out of an idea or thought in mind. Form follows thought. And, I ascribe to the belief that we were created in the likeness of the Divine Source of All that Is, which is *magnificent*—not ordinary. So, it is that we are made of that same magnificence at the essence of our own being.

Together we created a powerful vision statement for Charlene from the inside out: *I am an angel of universal Love, embodying healing and growth and inspiring higher awareness.*

Then, I declared, "Charlene, your only purpose in life is to *be* that, so what will you *do* that will empower you to *be* the angel of Universal Love that you are?"

We co-created her purpose statement: *My purpose is to joyously share my Self, my skills and my gifts, honor wholeness, and celebrate freedom!*

We also discovered her key values, guiding principles, and highest aspirations. With that framework in place, we designed a holistic MasterPlan that included goals and action steps—all with the intention of supporting her to manifest her "vision and purpose" in every aspect of her life.

Within three months of experiencing that process, Charlene had quit her part-time job, filled her calendar with hypnotherapy clients, and started marketing a public workshop titled, "Discovering Your Psychic Abilities." She was clear about who she was, from the inside out, and what she wanted. She had a plan and she was in action working her plan.

Her friends noticed a difference and asked, "What happened to you?" So *my* phone started ringing with people asking me to facilitate that process with them! Honestly, it wasn't until I was in the middle of facilitating it for the third time that the light bulb turned on in my mind. I realized *this* as my vocation of destiny.

By the way, five years later Charlene had her own public television show as a psychic. People were calling in live and consulting with her on the air.

Today, there are Six Steps to the Living Your Vision® process:

1. Discover: Who am I?
2. Clarify: What do I want?

3. Create a plan
4. Work my plan
5. Review my plan routinely
5. Utilize support

You'll recognize the first four. They are powerful and they are *transformational*, because they empower the individual from the inside out. I was inspired to add steps five and six to the process when I began noticing a phenomenon that was consistent with each one of those initial clients. After a few months, they stopped working their plan and they let it gather dust on the shelf. The momentum of breakthroughs and miracles slowed down and then stopped. The result was as if he or she had taken their foot off the accelerator.

I designed follow-up coaching sessions to assist my clients in establishing empowering habits that would support them in staying conscious of their intentions, on track, and measuring progress toward their goals. One of those key habits was to review their plan routinely to keep it current and alive in their consciousness. With these success factors in place, they began to develop self-empowering habits that would serve their lifetime.

For me, the transformational power of their self-empowerment reminded me of the ancient Chinese proverb about the difference between handing people fish to eat versus teaching them to fish for themselves.

Let's take a deeper look at the elements of the Living Your Vision ® process.

Step One. Discover: Who Am I? (Inside Out)

> "IT IS ONLY WITH THE HEART THAT ONE CAN SEE RIGHTLY; WHAT IS ESSENTIAL IS INVISIBLE TO THE EYE."
> ~ Antione de Saint-Exupery

Vision: your *Being*. In this first phase of step one, we discover the essence of who you are, the highest idea of yourself at your core, an expression of your divinity. This is the unalterable truth of you, regardless of the circumstances. We begin your vision statement with the powerful words "I Am." These words are translated into English from the sound of the "Om" in Sanskrit, which is the highest human expression of the divine Source, meaning "God in Action."

We choose to begin with "I Am" because our words are pure energy. They have enormous power. What we speak, we manifest, just as the Hebrew word "davar" means both "word" and "thing." And, we mindfully choose the words that follow, so we are calling forth the highest and the best of ourselves.

The inside out vision process taps into inner wisdom and unleashes personal power and passion. According to the dictionary, vision is a consistently held mental image of a possible reality. You are said to have "realized your vision" when reality has become what you have envisioned. I suggest that you realize your inner vision when you have claimed it as your truth, you *own* it, and you are manifesting it in life.

> "A BILLION STARS GO SPINNING THROUGH THE NIGHT,
> BLAZING HIGH ABOVE YOUR HEAD.
> BUT IN YOU IS THE PRESENCE THAT
> WILL BE, WHEN ALL THE STARS ARE DEAD."
> ~ RAINER MARIA RILKE

What is this profound and mysterious Presence the looks out through your eyes as you read these words and that knows that you know you are seeing? Cultivate this Presence as you move mindfully through your day!

Purpose: your *Doing*. Next, we discover what you *do* that empowers you to *be* who you are. There is only one purpose in life and that is to be who you are—to surrender to your divine design. What is important for you to do that empowers you to be the essence of who you are? What are the fundamental actions you must take that effectively empower the manifestation of your essence—so that, when you are *doing* what you do, you are showing up as your essence, *being* authentically **you**!

For example, when Charlene is joyously sharing her self, honoring her wholeness, and celebrating freedom, she is experiencing herself as an angel of universal love, embodying healing, growth and inspiring higher awareness. And, that is how she is showing up for others!

Values: Then we discover *how* you will honor your vision and purpose. What qualities of intrinsic worth do you choose to honor that most effectively support you in experiencing quality of life? For example: Integrity, Spirituality, Intimacy, Freedom, Joy, Gratitude, Abundance, Vitality, Honesty, Balance, Connection, Excellence, Accomplishment, Nature, Family, Health, Learning, Growth, and Play.

I ascribe to this notion: quality of life is directly related to the extent that you honor your values. They are powerful benchmarks for making decisions, and become lenses to look through to discover what is working or not working for you. Values are guideposts for making changes. The more fully I honor my values, the more ease and freedom, satisfaction, and fulfillment I experience in my life.

Step Two. Clarify: What Do I Want? (Inside Out)

"DO NOT ALLOW YOUR LIFE TO REPRESENT ANYTHING BUT THE GRANDEST VERSION OF THE GREATEST VISION YOU EVER HAD ABOUT WHO YOU ARE." ~ NEALE DONALD WALSCH

What are your dreams, goals, passions, desires, and yearnings; what are the things you *love* and love to do? We discover what your *heart* wants. We consult your heart, not your head. Your head and your heart were designed to work in partnership and your heart was designed to lead the dance. Once you have accessed your heart's desires, then your head gets to do what it does best: design and execute the plan.

So, we send your head on vacation and create a sacred space for your heart to play. Instead of designing goals (that word carries too much baggage from an old paradigm of "have to," and "should"), we discover your *choices*:

C = Choosing
H = Heart-centered
O = Opportunities, that are:
I = Inspiring
C = Congruent
E = Empowering
S = Specific and measurable

1998 © LYV Enterprises, Inc. Permission to copy granted

Step Three. Create a Plan (Inside Out)

"IF YOU HAVE BUILT CASTLES IN THE AIR, YOUR WORK NEED NOT BE LOST; THAT IS WHERE THEY SHOULD BE. NOW PUT THE FOUNDATIONS UNDER THEM!" ~ HENRY DAVID THOREAU

Together we design a MasterPlan that includes intentions, choices, and measurable action steps that are *all* focused on empowering your vision and purpose.

For example, here are my vision and purpose statements:

I Am Divine Inspiration, lovingly and powerfully calling forth essence into action and extraordinary expression.

My purpose is to enthusiastically let Divine Love and Light express through my body, my mind, and my spirit.

My Intention for my physical body is to celebrate the full expression of my body.

One of my choices for my physical body is to enjoy freedom and vitality with my body weight stabilized at 135 pounds by December 1st.

My action steps are:

- Eat only foods that are prepared with love.
- Include at least 10% protein in my breakfast, lunch and dinner.
- Include at least 80% vegetables for breakfast, lunch and dinner.
- Savor one delicious serving of whole grain bread per week.
- Maintain daily vitamins and minerals – morning and bedtime.

- Enjoy my two mile power walks in nature at least three times a week.
- Jump on my rebounder for a minimum of 10 minutes at least five times a week.

Other choices that support the achievement of my intention address my sexuality, personal grooming, stress management, medical maintenance, recreation, and play.

My action steps are designed to empower my intentions and choices, and my intentions and choices are designed to empower my vision and purpose, so that I *feel* the fulfillment of being **on** purpose every moment of every day—whether I am indulging in a bubble bath or making a presentation to a prospective client.

Step Four. Work My Plan (Inside Out)

> "THE COURAGE TO FOLLOW OUR DREAMS IS THE FIRST
> STEP TOWARD DESTINY." ~ UNKNOWN

This is where the rubber hits the road. This is not just *admiring* the accomplishment of that beautiful completed MasterPlan full of great intentions. This is not just *talking* about working the plan. This is about putting the plan into action. Taking the actions steps. Being in *motion*.

This is where inertia is confronted. This is where resistance shows up. This is where we hit the familiar obstacles to making changes in our lives. All the reasons and excuses and fears show up, along with the belief they are real that stops us. The opportunity is to make a different choice that calls forth our essential qualities *and* everything we want to manifest in our lives.

Elizabeth was in her late 50's. She had earned three Ph.Ds and when she contracted for her Living Your Vision® process, she said, "Fran, I have been a student all my life. It is time to do something viable in the world." Yes, Elizabeth was a life long learner *and* she was driven to learn by a belief that she was never good enough.

We discovered her Vision and Purpose: *I am a pure expression of Divine Will in the World, recognized as love and wisdom, embodying truth, beauty, and goodness.*

My purpose is to serve the Divine Plan/humanity/planet by sharing myself authentically, to follow the guidance of my heart, trusting the process with joy and gratitude.

Elizabeth had a four-drawer filing cabinet crammed full of ideas for what she wanted to do when she grew up. With the clarity of her vision and purpose, we discovered the most compelling and passionate expressions of Divine Will dwelling in her heart.

She had three lofty life goals: 1. To be an internationally renowned public speaker. 2. To help business owners in the Soviet Union learn how to manage in the New World market, utilizing her knowledge of organizational development. 3. With a heart for the plight of the Tibetan people, she wanted to help them save their culture.

Elizabeth was willing to give herself ten years to achieve these goals. Within ten *months* of embodying her vision and purpose, and being in action, she realized all three goals. After a lifetime of never good enough, holding back, hiding out behind the books, and stuffing a filing cabinet, Elizabeth took one first step into action, and that step precipitated a whole stream of miraculous events unforeseen from behind the filing cabinet.

At the end of ten months, she had been to Russia, she had met with the Dalai Lama in India, and she had spoken at the National Futurists Conference. And, it all happened magically for her. Then she said, "Okay Fran, what's next?" So we designed a new plan with new choices, all focused on empowering her vision and purpose. Her vision and purpose hadn't changed, but she was embodying higher aspects of her essence and was living in a New World of possibilities.

Step Five. Review My Plan Routinely (Inside Out)

"To put the world right in order, we must first put the
nation in order; to put the nation in order, we must first
put the family in order; to put the family in order, we must
first cultivate our personal life; we must first set our
hearts right." ~ Confucius

Develop the habit of routinely reviewing your plan with
the intention of evaluating your intentions, choices, and
actions. Within the context of your vision, purpose, and
values, check yourself with questions like these:

- Is this my truth today?
- What is working? What is not working?
- What will I give myself permission to change?
- What will I let go of?
- What have I accomplished? What will I celebrate or
  acknowledge?
- What's next?

Keep your plan alive and juicy with excitement and *feeling*
for what you want. Utilize it consistently like a favorite tool.

Some of my clients create a sacred time for themselves
weekly to review their MasterPlan and to plan their week.
They mark their calendar and keep that appointment with
themselves with the same level of integrity they would hold
for appointments with their own clients. Why? Because they
have learned that this practice supports them in staying on
track and getting back on track sooner, whenever they fall
off; for measuring and celebrating their success, and learning
from their failures; for staying true to themselves and
experiencing a greater measure of satisfaction and fulfillment.

Step Six. Utilize Support

"Too often we underestimate the power of a touch, a smile,
a kind word, a listening ear, an honest compliment, or the
smallest act of caring, all of which have the potential to
turn a life around." ~ Leo Buscaglia

One of the first questions I ask a new Living Your Vision® client is, "How many people can you name who will support, champion, and celebrate the changes you want to make for yourself?" If my client can't name more than two people (and their coach, *me*, is one of the two), I say that is not enough!

Having a coach is a very powerful support structure. Still, I recommend clients build a broader base of support to augment their relationship with a coach. This is a success factor for making significant life changes and assists in accelerating client progress. I have worked with many clients over the years that were in various stages of leaving toxic work environments or dead-end intimate relationships. Without support or understanding in the environment that they wanted to leave, it was critically important to have other relationships to turn to for support.

John

John's vision and purpose statements: *I Am a colorful glowing expression of pure love, a messenger and the message.*

My purpose is to love unconditionally, recognizing that we are One; creating beauty, being happy, sharing my gifts joyfully, and celebrating Life daily.

When John started working with me he was disorganized, unfocused, and inconsistent with his personal habits. He was in the business of selling cellular phones at the time, averaging about three a month; he was not earning a living.

After the first three months that he worked with me, he began selling an average of thirty cell phones a month. With the assistance of the coaching, John was able to see what wasn't working about his personal habits and what it was costing in the quality of his life. For example, he would make two different appointments across town from each other and leave **no** time in his planner for the travel time to get from one to the other. He was always running late! That was costing him credibility with his customers and affecting his self-esteem and his self-respect. He decided that he wanted to be on time for his appointments. So, we designed a structure right into his planner that reminded him every day to leave at least an hour between appointments. Practicing new habits like that one supported him in producing the results he wanted.

What John tells his friends about what he values the most about the Living Your Vision® process is not about the cell phones. In the process of discovering his essence of "pure love," *owning that,* and living in alignment with it, he healed his relationship with his father.

His parents would not come to his home because of their judgment about his "alternative" lifestyle; they would not accept it. Out of learning that his purpose is to love unconditionally, he realized the importance of his relationship with his parents. John wrote them a letter and let them know that he accepted them just the way they are and understood that they had a hard time accepting his choice, and that he didn't need to change that. And he expressed his love for them. As a result of that letter, his parents decided to take a vacation. They drove to the city where he lived and actually came to his home and met the man that he lives with.

They had a wonderful, loving visit and expressed their love for each other. His father died while driving back home.

Because John had experienced completion with his father, he could more easily accept his father's unexpected death. The miracle of healing resulted from John "*being* the colorful glowing expression of purest love, the messenger and the message. And *loving* unconditionally." He was *Living his Vision.*

The Living Your Vision ® Inside Out Model

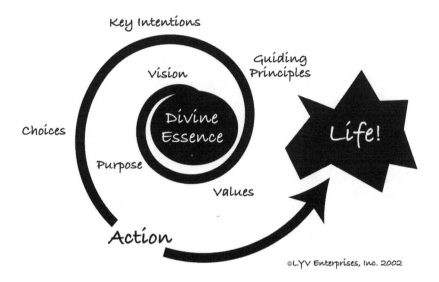

©LYV Enterprises, Inc. 2002

Miracles

"WE ALL HAVE THE EXTRAORDINARY CODED WITHIN US...
WAITING TO BE RELEASED." ~ JEAN HOUSTON

David's vision statement: *I Am the graceful power and freedom of a soaring eagle.* David was a new chiropractor just launching his first practice. When David embodied his vision and purpose, he grew his business 150% within six months while balancing his personal sports and hobby interests and his family time.

Caroline's vision statement: *I Am simply elegant, graceful, a peony, ritual of joy, serene peace, radiating energy, music of the universe, and living meditation.* Caroline bailed out of a toxic corporate environment and created a garden in her back yard that nurtures her soul and brings her year-round pleasure.

Ann's vision statement: *I Am the flowering vine, spiraling upward toward the light, moving with purpose and joy.* Ann left the corporation she was working for, started her own company, and made triple the income within one year as an independent contractor for the same company.

Wanda's vision statement: *I Am a visionary integrator, a powerful, nurturing influence for transformation.* Wanda transformed herself from a vice president-level Human Resources Director of a national HMO to her highly successful private executive coaching practice.

Paula's vision statement: *I Am the unbound light of creative possibilities, an orchestrator and synthesizer, calling forth the Higher Heart of human consciousness.* Paula significantly increased her level of fulfillment in her general manager position with a non-profit association and she transformed her relationship with her husband, and her physical, emotional, and spiritual well-being.

More examples of compelling Vision and Purpose statements for your inspiration:

I AM a shimmering sprite, bearer of God-Light, a presence of joy, beauty, and reverence for all Life.

My purpose is to honor my Soul-Self by celebrating Life, staying grounded and centered and open to guidance.

~ Office Manager

I AM a being of Light, radiating a powerful healing force from the center of knowledge; I Am wise without thought; Mighty without effort; Ancient beyond time.

My purpose is to follow my bliss; to purposefully seek wisdom through learning and intuitive knowledge, sharing it freely with all. *~ School Principal*

I AM a powerful goddess of ancient wisdom and healing, radiating natural beauty, gentle strength, and compassion.

My purpose is to Trust and to Love unconditionally; to embody centeredness and balance; to provide opportunities for freedom, creativity, and wholeness for all. ~ Massage Therapist

I AM the joyous expression of the Love of God.
My purpose is to relax and giggle; let go and have fun!
                                                    ~ *Life Coach*

I AM Cosmic Golden Dancer, Deep Loving Connection, and an Artist of the Invisible, dancing in the glow of Spirit, at peace with what I know and holding a caring space for Discovery, Transformation, and Joy.

My purpose is to embrace process...trust, accept, and powerfully reflect what I see and know, and call forth the unconscious into awareness, connecting humanity with spirit and opening hearts to love.
                                              ~ *Leadership Coach*

We are each being called to a new level of consciousness. We are journeying through this experience called life with the ability and opportunity to choose mediocrity, toleration, and resignation, or fulfillment, incredible aliveness, and authentic joy. Miracles are the norm when we live our vision from the inside out. I believe in the possibility of a shift in the quality of life on earth as we each claim our magnificence and live it passionately. We are each a contribution to the consciousness that uplifts the whole web of being.

How would your life be different if you lived it from the inside out? What action will you commit to that will empower you in *living* your vision?

"OUR DEEPEST FEAR IS NOT THAT WE ARE INADEQUATE. OUR DEEPEST FEAR IS THAT WE ARE POWERFUL BEYOND MEASURE."
                          ~ MARIANNE WILLIAMSON

About
Fran Fisher

Fran Fisher is President of LYV Enterprises, Inc. and its division, Academy for Coach Training. She is founder of *Living Your Vision®*, a process for empowering individuals in transforming their visions into reality, a visionary leader, an international speaker, and a Master Certified Coach (MCC). Fran serves on the Advisory Board of the Association for Coach Training Organizations (ACTO), and was chair of the Credentialing Committee of the *International Coach Federation* (ICF), a board member of the ICF, as well as a charter member and treasurer for the *Professional & Personal Coaches Association* (PPCA).

Fran's passion is providing inspired guidance, support, and coaching, as well as helping people liberate their personal power and manifest their highest visions. As a master coach, she works with visionary leaders, helping them fulfill the desires of their hearts. She blends the art of visioning, the structure of planning, and her intuitive ability to empower and guide clients to success and fulfillment.

In 1991 Fran founded the *Living Your Vision® (LYV)* process, and in 1994 she launched the Licensing and Certification Program for coaches to deliver this process. LYV coaches nationwide are now working with people of all ages in all walks of life, such as art, health, communication, education, consulting, counseling, therapy, sales, government, etc.

In 1997, Fran founded the Academy for Coach Training, a comprehensive Coach Training and Certification program with an extraordinary transformational coaching model— *coaching from the Inside Out*.

Prior to 1991, Fran augmented her corporate career as a national real estate Marketing Director by achieving the distinction of Certified Property Manager (CPM) with the Institute of Real Estate Management. She attended a long list of continuing education and personal growth courses to enhance her intuitive and coaching skills. In 1995, she earned her *Certified Personal and Professional Coach* designation with The Coaches Training Institute in San Rafael, California, and her *Master Certified Coach* designation from the International Coach Federation in 1998.

Living in Bellevue, WA, Fran is a contributing author to the Simon and Schuster best seller *Chocolate For A Woman's Soul*, and is currently writing her book about the *Living Your Vision*® process. In her leisure time she enjoys her grandchildren, gardening, ballroom dancing, being in nature and long walks on ocean beaches.

To contact Fran, call (425) 401-0309, E-mail her at fran@coachtraining.com, or visit her website at www.coachtraining.com.

Are Your Limiting Beliefs Affecting Your Vision?

By Diane Cunningham

As a coach, I have partnered with many clients to create a vision for their life. What I've discovered is that with focus and intent, most clients can find clarity about their vision in a short time. However, they have much more difficulty implementing that vision into their daily lives. Why is this the case? My experience indicates that the difficulty is because of the limiting beliefs that those clients carry with them. In this chapter, I will share with you how to recognize and then overcome limiting beliefs that are holding you back from seeing your clear, compelling vision become reality.

The first step to overcoming your limiting beliefs is to understand just what that term means. A **limiting belief** is a thought or value that stands in the way of you moving forward or that gets in the way of what you want in life. Marcia Wieder, author of *Making Your Dreams Come True* says that a belief is an assumption you have; a way of looking at things that determines your choices. Dr. Phil McGraw, Ph.D. says, "Fixed beliefs reflect your overall understanding of your place in the world. They are fixed because you are no longer adding or subtracting new information; they are perceptions that have been rigid and unchanging... They influence every value you have, your perceptions or your basic worth as a human being, and your core traits and characteristics. They tell you where your boundaries are. They contain your expectations about what ought to happen in your life."

According to Dilts, Hallbom & Smith in their book, *Beliefs: Pathways to Health & Well-Being*, belief system issues often occur around situations involving change. Beliefs and expectations about outcomes and your personal capabilities play an important role in the change process. Limiting beliefs are internal terrorists that sabotage your best efforts. You can't arrest these terrorists because they are part of you. Rather than destroying them, they need to be involved in the solution. These obstructions can represent the part of you that doesn't want to change or the part of you that doesn't know how to change.

Let's look at some of the components of Belief Systems:

- **Outcome Expectancy**: You believe that your goal is achievable. If you do not believe the goal or outcome is possible, then you experience **hopelessness and inaction**.

- **Self-Efficacy Expectancy**: You believe that your goal is possible and that you have whatever it takes to reach your goal. If you think that others can achieve their goals, but not you, you don't have self–efficacy, and you have **helplessness and inaction**.

- **Worthlessness:** You believe that you don't deserve your goal because of something you are or have or haven't done, and you experience **hopelessness and inaction.**

- **Hopelessness + Helplessness = Apathy**: Apathy moves you away from your vision.

Self-efficacy beliefs and expectations can be major blocks to how much effort you will use and how long you will be able to cope in dealing with a stressful situation. If you are unsure about your ability to control your behaviors, you may tend to undermine your efforts. Relapsing to previous behaviors is common for individuals when their coping skills are taxed and they disbelieve their ability to be successful. You change your behavior by acquiring new experiences and developing new frames of reference and skills.

Jeff is a good example of Outcome and Self-Efficacy Expectancy. He came to see me because he wanted more balance in this life. He was an accountant and it was tax time. He wanted to have fun in his life and spend quality time with his wife. During our initial conversation, he said that he felt stuck, hopeless, and helpless. He didn't feel that his vision was possible because he had tried several different avenues that hadn't worked out for him. He saw other accountants around him maintaining balance in their lives. Why couldn't he? He was discouraged and apathetic about his wife and children and life in general. He was seeing a doctor because he had no energy and was having short-term memory loss. He felt like he also needed a coach to help him get a new perspective on life and to be able to move his life forward. We will discuss Jeff more later in the chapter.

Beliefs are not necessarily based on a logical framework of ideas and aren't intended to coincide with reality. Another interesting concept about beliefs comes from Lynn Grabhorn, who wrote the book *Excuse Me, Your Life is Waiting*. She states that humans are electromagnetic *beings* and that we draw things into our lives (magnetize) by controlling the feelings that come from thoughts and beliefs. Feelings go out from us like electromagnetic waves looking for the same frequency vibrations. If you think negative feelings, you are sending negative vibrations. You must focus on what you want, not on what you don't want. By focusing on what you want, those things will come to you by the Law of Attraction. Lynn's strategy is to:

1. Identify what you don't want.
2. Identify what you do want.
3. Get into the feeling place.
4. Expect, listen, and allow the things you do want to happen.

How Do You Recognize Limiting Beliefs?

Most limiting beliefs are unconscious and hard to define because they are part of everyday life. Have you ever heard someone say, "This is crazy and doesn't make sense, but…" or "It just isn't like me; I don't understand it." If you've heard something similar, you have a clue about how limiting beliefs are affecting the speaker. The language seems to be focused on what the person can or can't do, should or shouldn't do, or ought or ought not to do.

Another way to identify beliefs is by finding a problem situation that you have unsuccessfully tried to change. For instance, you might ask yourself the following questions:

- "What does it mean about me that I haven't been able to change this?"
- "What stops me from having it now?"

These questions help you do inward introspection and find answers. Some common unresolved limiting beliefs are:

- I am not good enough to be successful.
- I don't have knowledge in that subject.
- I am just not technical.
- I worry what people will think.
- I am too old to go back to school.
- I don't have time to do that.
- I missed my opportunity years ago.
- I don't trust myself or anyone else.
- I have to work hard to make money.
- I can't be spiritual and have money.
- If I get what I want then I will lose something else.

To illustrate limiting beliefs and language patterns, let me share a personal story. I was attending my second course at the Academy for Coaches Training in Seattle. In class we were working on an empowerment process with a partner. The class had an uneven number of students, so I had the opportunity to work with one of the course facilitators. I explained to my partner that I had been in Nursing Education and Management most of my career and had mentored and coached individuals all my professional life. Before attending the training, I thought that I didn't need to be a Certified Coach because I thought I had learned the content and skills from various other training classes and numerous certifications in nursing and complementary medicine. But I knew I would benefit from more coaching classes, so I convinced my hospital to send me to the first two sessions of the coaches training. At the training, I complained to my class partner that the hospital wouldn't send me to the rest of the training to become a Certified Coach due to hard times in healthcare, which caused lost jobs, reduced money for training, etc.

At this point my partner stopped me and said six words that changed my life: "Diane, you aren't holding yourself big." I thought to myself, "You are right." My limiting belief was that I felt powerless to change the environment/culture. My partner had opened up another option or point of view for me. I went back home feeling empowered. I wrote a proposal to the hospital to pay for the rest of my coach training and stated all the benefits to the hospital. The proposal went through three layers of management to be signed. When it was signed, I partnered with the Human Resource Department to set up a coaching program for our hospital, which is still in existence today.

Being a Holistic Health Practitioner and Coach, clients are drawn to me to be coached around health goals in relation to their vision (I always make sure that they are seeing a physician if they have serious health issues). Some common language patterns that I hear in my practice are:

- I don't get any support.
- I can't get them off of my back.
- I made a rash decision.
- He gives me a pain in the neck.
- I don't want to look at the problem.
- Nothing seems clear to me.
- I am dying to find out what happens.
- I'm always holding back.
- I have one headache after another.

When I work with a client and we identify the language pattern she or he is using, I invite her or him to change or reframe it to something more positive.

Where Do Limiting Beliefs Come From?

Our decisions and choices result from attitudes and beliefs that we have developed since the day that we were born. Most of the limiting beliefs fall into the following categories:

Parents: Early in our childhood we heard statements from our parents such as, " I will love you if you clean your room," or " Be a good girl and make your bed." We got the idea that we were loved only if we did certain things. But in reality these things had nothing to do with our deep, inner self-worth. Other statements that can have long lasting imprints include, "You will never make anything of your self," or "Who do you think you are?" or "Women aren't supposed to do that." Our beliefs and values are formed at a very early age, and these early messages may have affected our negative self-talk.

Friends: Our peer group makes lasting impressions on us. For instance, my cousin was on steroids for a rare illness. These steroids caused her to gain a lot of weight. She had never been heavy before and had been, in fact, very petite. But a boy at her school told her that she was fat. My cousin is now in remission from her disease and is petite again, but she still thinks she is fat and has been treated for bulimia. How powerful words are. The subconscious mind doesn't know the difference between reality and non-reality. We must let our mind hear and re-frame the negative thoughts.

Teachers: I have worked with many clients to re-frame limiting beliefs that were caused from what teachers told them 30 years ago. Somehow we take these casual comments that were made to us when we were young and code them as negative. "You will never graduate from high school," "You just don't have what it takes to go to college," or "You are not an artist."

Traumatic Experiences: As we all know, traumatic experiences are common place and vary in the degree of severity. What is interesting is that we respond to them differently. For example, Lance Armstrong, Tour de France winner and author of the book, *It's Not About the Bike*, had testicular cancer. Instead of taking a victim position, as someone with limiting beliefs might do, he took charge of his life and overcame his disease. He won the Tour de France four times after his recovery. However, what was important to him was that he was a cancer survivor.

How Do We Change Limiting Beliefs?

Patricia Cota Robles stated, "What we think about, what we hold in our minds and put our attention and energy into, we actually draw into our lives. So it is time to stop precipitating the things that we don't want and start drawing in the things to ourselves, the things that we do want."

We are what we focus on. Energy flows where attention goes. If you focus on the negative, that is what you are going to get. Keeping all that in mind, I have my clients say "**Stop**" when they experience negative self-talk or negative thoughts. Then I invite them to envision a pleasant place in nature that they love, and to immerse fully into that place by focusing on what they are seeing, feeling, hearing, smelling, and tasting. Using this technique frequently helps to break the negative thought patterns and self-talk so that the clients can focus on their visions.

You might think changing beliefs to be difficult, effortful, or that it will take focus, determination, commitment, concentration, and discipline. In actuality, you naturally and spontaneously change hundreds of beliefs during your lifetime. Robert Dilts believes that according to the theory of self-organization, beliefs change through a destabilization process. Your New Belief may be brought forth easily and effortlessly without conflict. The system may re-stabilize itself around a new point of balance or reference point. This happened in my personal example when six words changed or re-framed my perspective and ultimately my belief about being powerless.

Many limiting beliefs are a result of fear. A paradox in life is that facing fear requires looking at change, a process that causes fear in nearly all of us. Marcia Wieder talks about a tips jar at a restaurant that says, "If you fear change, leave it here." The reality is that the fear may not even revolve around what is being changed. Your fear might actually be a limiting belief about the body's ability to handle the act of changing.

We think of fear filled with dark unknowns, with the ultimate fear being a feeling of death. Change is the Old You dying away, allowing you to be transformed. Facing your fear by being clear about what you want will often release the part of you that no longer fits so you can move forward toward your vision. Distinguish between restricting fears such as unsafe situations versus a fear of the change that might be limiting you.

When you really think about it, we are creatures of change. Look at all the changes you have gone through since childhood, adolescence, and stages of adulthood. Isn't change part of the cycle of nature?

Louise Hay presented it beautifully when she said:

A New Belief is planted in the SPRING
The seed grows in the SUMMER where it matures,
becomes strong, and takes root
In the AUTUMN the belief becomes outdated
and withers, its purpose served.
Positive intentions and purposes are harvested and
separated from the parts that are no longer necessary.
In the WINTER parts of the belief no longer needed
fade away.

I encourage my clients to look at the positive intention of their negative belief before they discard it. Can they meet that positive intention through other thoughts or activities?

What is the lesson to be learned? My experience has been that if we don't learn the lesson that life is trying to teach us, it will keep showing up in different forms until we get it.

Belief Audit

When working with my clients, if I hear a negative belief or language pattern, I have my client fill out the Belief Self-Assessment Sheet, which was developed by the NLP World Health Community for the 21st Century.

Belief Self-Assessment Sheet

Write down a one sentence description of the vision or outcome you would like to achieve:

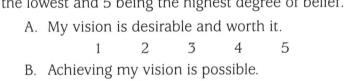

Rate your degree of belief in your vision in relation to each of the statements on a scale of 1 to 5, with 1 being the lowest and 5 being the highest degree of belief.

A. My vision is desirable and worth it.
       1   2   3   4   5

B. Achieving my vision is possible.
       1   2   3   4   5

C. What I have to do in order to achieve my vision is clear, appropriate, and ecological.
       1   2   3   4   5

D. I have the capabilities necessary to achieve my vision.
       1   2   3   4   5

E. I deserve to achieve my vision.
       1   2   3   4   5

Let me explain the process I use with my clients using this assessment. If the client rates himself or herself three or below on any of these questions, then we work together to discuss each area to see where this limiting belief came from. At this point, I use one of several strategies to work with limiting beliefs. If the client chooses to resolve the limiting belief, then we move forward to reframe the belief into a more positive belief. I use this strategy when I feel that the belief isn't deep seated and could be re-framed fairly easily. Jeff, from my previous example, rated himself a three or below on: "It is possible to achieve my vision; What I have to do in order to achieve my vision is clear, appropriate, and ecological; and I have the capabilities necessary to achieve my vision."

The strategy is to have the client identify what his or her old belief is. Then I have the client identify what he or she wants the New Belief to be and write it down as a one sentence affirmation. We may do brainstorming here to become totally clear about the New Belief.

Next, we do a creative visualization where the client imagines a pleasant place in nature, which is usually a garden of his or her own creation. I ask them to look for a symbol that represents the Old Belief (for example, a dead tree, statue, etc.). I ask the client to pretend to step into that symbol and experience it fully. I ask, "What does it look like? Where does the feeling reside in your body? Is there a voice? What is it saying? Is there a smell? Is there a taste?" Then I ask the client to look around the garden to find a symbol that represents the New Belief and experience that symbol fully. I have the client say his or her New Belief to see if it needs any tweaking. Then I ask the client to return from the garden with the symbol that represents the New Belief. I then invite the client to look for a sticker or picture in real life that represents the symbol of the New Belief. I instruct the client to place the picture in obvious places (bedroom clock, bathroom mirror, refrigerator, car steering wheel, or wallet, etc.) as a reminder of the New Belief.

Let's continue with the story of Jeff, the accountant. When he went to the garden, his limiting belief symbol was a large, black bowling ball. He felt discomfort in his chest. There was a voice that said, "I have no energy. I can't remember the numbers." The garden smelled like death and there was a nasty taste in his mouth. His symbol for the New Belief was a huge flower garden with a wide variety of brilliantly colored flowers. There was a voice that said, "You can have fun in your life. You are at peace." The entire garden smelled delightful with the combination of scents. He had a pleasant taste in his mouth. He felt energized and totally refreshed.

Jeff now has a picture of a huge flower garden on the wall in front of his desk so that he can connect with his New Belief several times a day. In partnering with him through the visioning process, we found that he wasn't clear about his vision. His new vision included helping others. This materialized in his life by hiring other accountants to do the day-to-day operations of his business, while he did what he loved to do—consult with small business owners and teach classes. And he is definitely having more fun in his life by traveling to places he has always wanted to visit with his wife.

The second strategy I use takes the client to the Museum of Old Beliefs, from the *Thought Inoculation Process* created by Robert Dilts. In our lives we've all changed many of our beliefs. One of my beliefs I had when I was teenager was that girls with pierced ears were loose women, so I never had my ears pierced. But it was very fashionable to wear pierced earrings, so when I was 36 years-old I threw this old belief into the Museum of Old Beliefs and got my ears pierced.

A few other common beliefs are:
- You can't go swimming after eating.
- After 40 you will need to wear reading glasses.
- I always have jet lag after a long trip.
- Relationships take a lot of work.

I ask my client to think of an old belief that he or she once had, and then discarded, as it no longer served them. They usually think of at least one or two. Next, I have the client get very clear about their limiting belief and feel it fully (for example, "What does it look like? Where does the feeling reside in their body? Is there is a voice? What is it saying? Is there a smell? Is there is a taste?"). Finally, I partner with the client to get very clear about the New Belief using the same process as above. Then I take him or her through the following process (see diagram below).

1. Start by stating the limiting belief. Feel the limiting belief fully as mentioned above.

2. Step into a place where there is doubt about the limiting belief (remind the client that they have doubted other beliefs before).

3. When the client thinks of the limiting belief that they once held and simply doesn't believe anymore, they are ready to step into the Museum of Old Beliefs. (What does it look like? Have the client describe it fully.)

Thought Inoculation Process*

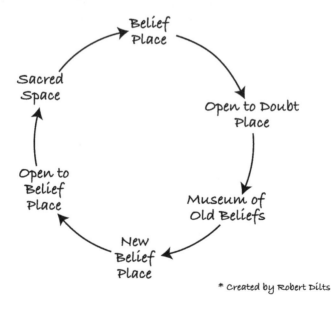

* Created by Robert Dilts

4. Leave the Old Belief there.

5. The client states the New Belief. What does the New Belief look like? Where does the feeling reside in their body? Is there a voice? What is it saying? Is there a smell? Is there a taste?

6. I have the client say the New Belief to make sure that they are comfortable with the wording. If not I have them work with it until it feels good on all levels.

7. Then the client steps into the place where they are open to believing the New Belief.

8. Now the client thinks of their New Belief as something they wouldn't violate, something that they feel so strongly about that they wouldn't hesitate to defend it—a Sacred Space. In this Sacred Space have them say their New Belief and connect with spirit. Check to see how the New Belief feels on all levels after connecting with spirit.

9. Finally have the client step back into the Old Belief place to test the New Belief. Usually the client will not remember what the Old Belief was and feels very elated about the New Belief.

I used this process with a client named Mary. Her vision statement was: "I am an innovative, intuitive, passionate, transformational healer who dances in the essence of spirit, abundance, joy, and health." All the words seemed congruent for Mary except for the word "abundance." She had limiting beliefs about abundance due to the statements that her father made to her as a child. Clearly Mary needed to deal with her limiting beliefs before she could fully embrace her vision. Mary had three limiting beliefs about money:

- "I am born to a bondage of poverty through the lineage of women in my family."
- "I am inadequate, uninformed, and incapable in the presence of money."
- "Money is evil."

When Mary spoke of these beliefs she was hunched over. She pictured herself like a prisoner in chains. A voice called "Sir" was providing negative self-talk. She felt discouraged and had an energy vortex in the palms of her hands. When she went to the Museum of Old Beliefs, she felt it was like the hull of a ship—dark, dusty, and musty. She had a bitter taste in her mouth. She was relieved and happy to leave her old belief there with many other old beliefs that she had discarded long ago.

We started the process with her New Belief: "I have abundance in all areas of my life with knowledge, understanding, and appreciation of what the Universe provides and in honor of spirit." She took her New Belief to the Open to Believe space. "Sir" had been transformed from an unkempt, unshaven individual to a clean-cut person who looked like one of her sons. "Sir" said, "God's speed" and kissed her on the left cheek. Mary, who represented the leader of the prisoners said, "I am free." The discomfort in her hands was gone. The room smelled like flowers and she had a sweet taste in her mouth. As she took her New Belief into the Sacred Space, she felt the spiritual connection and saw a rainbow of colored lights. When we checked the two remaining beliefs in the Old Belief space, they had been transformed as well. Mary was now ready to embrace her vision.

Mary is living her vision. She has a communications consulting business, although she is still growing both personally and professionally, which causes some chaos in her life. The rainbow connection symbol (as she calls it) that manifested itself during our work together is still with her three years later and validates to her that she is on the right track. Her belief about abundance has evolved to: "If you are prepared, clear about your intention for the highest good, the universe will provide at the level of abundance that you are ready to receive."

Secondary Gain

If I use the process to work with a client and the Old Belief still doesn't want to change, I usually ask the client, "What secondary gain are you getting from holding onto this belief?" I explain that secondary gain is the benefit or "payoff" you are getting from holding on to that limiting belief, behavior, or illness. Many of them say, "I am not getting any secondary gain." I ask them to go inside and ask their higher self for the secondary gain, and many times they will come up with answers such as:

- I would lose my wheelchair parking if I got better.
- It helps me keep my life in control.
- I would miss the attention that I get.
- I would have to have sex with my husband.
- I don't like my job.
- It gives me an opportunity to rest.
- I can hide from the world.
- I would have to do things that I don't want to do.

Secondary gain is deep-seeded in the subconscious and may take some time to find. Knowing the Old Belief and discovering what it has been getting for you is important. We wouldn't continue to hold on to a belief if it didn't get something for us. Some questions that I generally ask are: "What would your life be like without this belief? Would anything be missing?" " Does this belief either help you get something positive or help you avoid something?" What does having this belief allow you to do, to be, or to have?" The positive intention or secondary gain needs to be honored before the New Belief will work for you.

An example is a woman who is 30 pounds over weight and has a limiting belief that she doesn't have the will power to change her eating patterns. What might the secondary gain be here? It may keep her safe in her marriage and she is afraid that if she was thin and attractive, she may not stay faithful to her spouse. Another example may be a man who is not moving up in the company. He was afraid of the success that money can bring. He may believe that he is dishonoring his family as no one in his family had a college degree or prestigious position. This may also tie in to the limiting belief of worthlessness. "I don't deserve to have what I want."

Through the examples and stories presented in this chapter, we have discussed the importance of beliefs in getting what you want in life. Recognizing limiting beliefs and how they are developed is essential. Once the limiting beliefs have been identified and the secondary gains uncovered, you can utilize some of the strategies that I have mentioned to change those limiting beliefs to empowering beliefs. These new empowering beliefs will allow you to move forward along the path to stepping into your vision.

"MAY YOUR PATH BE CLEAR AND BRIGHT. MAY YOU EASILY AND EFFORTLESSLY STEP INTO YOUR VISION."
~ DIANE CUNNINGHAM

Secondary gain

Attention

Limiting belief
I don't finish anything — I give it 100% then get tired

About
Diane Cunningham

Diane Cunningham is a Certified Professional Coach and licensed Living Your Vision® Coach from the Academy for Coach Training in Seattle. Diane has collaborated with the Human Resources Department to set up the coaching program for the University of Utah Hospitals and Clinics in Salt Lake City, Utah. She currently coaches all levels of staff in achieving their work-related goals. She creatively balances her part time work as a Nurse Educator in Clinical Staff Education at the hospital and her private practice.

Diane's experience includes over thirty years in the health care industry holding positions of increasing responsibility in management, education, and marketing. She has an expertise in planning and implementing innovative health education programs. She has been an international speaker and has published several articles in the areas of community education, wellness, nursing leadership, and clinical nursing practices.

She recently spoke at the Sun Valley Wellness Conference on limiting beliefs in relation to health.

As a member of the health care team, Diane has developed an expertise in Integrative Complementary Medicine. She holds certifications in Health using Neurolingistic Programming, Hypnosis, Light Body Shamanic processes, Theta Healing, and is a Reiki Master. She mentors staff nurses in the use of Integrative Complementary Medicine in the hospital setting.

In her private practice, Diane uses her eclectic talents to partner with clients to reframe their limiting beliefs to enable them to reach their highest potential. She works with clients using the Living Your Vision® process to assist them in moving toward their vision. Diane also coaches clients in the areas of wellness and Magnetizing Abundance.

To contact Diane send an email to nlpgirl@aol.com.

Moving Beyond Fear to Find Your Vision

By Michele Molitor

Inspiration From Al

BOOM. I had hit a wall in my career. After being in the high tech industry for years, I was laid off from a job that was my career and my identity all rolled up into one. Losing my job hurt my pride and crushed my self-confidence. Feeling like a puddle of my former self, filled with fear, unknowing, and panic about what to do next, I went home and called my mom to tell her about my "bad" day. When I called, she sounded pretty upset, so I knew something was really wrong. She told me that our dear friend Al was probably going to die soon. His illness had taken a turn for the worse and it didn't look good at all.

In that moment, my perspective shifted dramatically. Here I was upset about being laid off from a job that had been a big part of my identity and role in the world, to find out that a close friend was dying. My day didn't seem so bad after all.

The next day I left to go on vacation with my entire family for a few days. I said to myself that I would take this time to rejuvenate my energy after the "painful breakup" with my job, and to start fresh upon my return. I declared to myself that the day after I returned would be the first day of the rest of my life and I would figure out what to do next. So, off I went to be with family and friends, and take some much needed rest and relaxation time.

I got home late Thursday night from my trip and was awakened early Friday morning by the phone. My father was calling to tell me that Al had passed away very early that morning. I was deeply saddened by the loss of my friend, and angry at the same time. You see Al didn't have to die so soon. He knew he was sick and refused to ask for help. He refused to let his fears show, to speak his truth, and live another day.

Al's death was a wake up call for me. It helped me see that life is too precious to waste it by hiding behind fears. That day I made a promise to Al, to myself, and to the universe, that I would never again live my life from a place of fear. It was too costly. Whatever those fears were, no matter how big, I would find a way to move through them and keep going.

And that's what I've done. I'm forever grateful to Al for being the catalyst and inspiration that helped me discover myself, my vision, *my* life.

> "IT IS A TERRIBLE THING TO SEE AND HAVE NO VISION."
>
> ~HELEN KELLER

Moving Through the Fear

To help me move through my own fears, I decided to hire a career coach, to help me figure out what was next. What I discovered was a whole new way of looking at things— a new vision and a new career.

The time I spent with my coach sent me on a journey. I began to see what assumptions I had made about myself and my career and how it was all "supposed" to look. I began to see things from a different perspective.

Through this process I was able to look more closely at my fears with an objective eye and see what they were actually made of. This closer examination gave me the courage to begin the movement through them and start to see the vision for my new career and my life.

I now have my own successful coaching company that gives me joy everyday as I help others find their own light creating the life and the work they love.

So what helped me make the leap? Going through the process of self-reflection to see what I wanted to build and what that foundation should be made of. This began by looking at my values and what was truly important to me. From there I was able to see things from different perspectives, see my fears for what they were, and get clear on what there was for me to do. From that whole and complete perspective, I was able to clearly identify and articulate my vision for myself and my company .

What is the light and the vision within you that is waiting to shine into the world? Through my experience, my wish for you is to find your own inspiration, move past your fears and step courageously into your vision. The world awaits!

"Your vision will become clear only when you look into your heart. Who looks outside dreams, who looks inside awakes." ~ Carl Jung

Values as Building Blocks

We all have things that we love to do. It may be cooking, or gardening, or mountain biking. Or it may be building things, developing something, or being of service to others. We might do these things for a living or as a volunteer or perhaps we don't even share those ideas or secret passions with other people. No matter what that activity is though, there most likely is a passion underneath it that keeps bringing you back to it. Somewhere deep within, those passions lie at your heart's core and are longing to be expressed.

"Everyone has been made for some particular work, and the desire for that work has been put in every heart."
~ Rumi

Inside of those passions are the values that make it so meaningful to you. It's these values that speak to the essence of who you are. What is your truth? What is important to you? What difference do you want to make in the world?

So how do you go about defining or realizing you own values? You must look into your own heart and see what your authentic self has to say—the unique expression of self that can only be given by you. Your core sets you apart from everyone else and is what will define your unique vision.

"THERE IS A VITALITY, A LIFE FORCE, AN ENERGY, A QUICKENING, THAT IS TRANSLATED THROUGH YOU INTO ACTION. BECAUSE THERE IS ONLY ONE OF YOU IN ALL TIME, THIS EXPRESSION IS UNIQUE. IF YOU BLOCK IT, IT WILL NEVER EXIST THROUGH ANY OTHER MEDIUM AND WILL BE LOST."

~MARTHA GRAHAM

Here are some questions to help clarify your values that will lay the foundation of your vision:

- What do you believe in?
- What are you willing to take a stand for?
- What do you bring to business?
- What will your work represent at the end of the day?
- What ethical lines are you not willing to cross no matter what the price?

The following partial list may also help you identify some of the values that are important to you. Use this list as a foundation to help recognize your own values, or add others to suit you as they surface.

Community	Loyalty	Connectedness
Love	Honesty	Generosity
Authenticity	Kindness	Success
Courage	Ethics	Creativity
Inspiration	Appreciation	Growth
Good deeds	Happiness	Wisdom
Warmth	Adventure	Contentment
Knowledge	Wealth	Security
Friendship	Empathy	Service
Good humor	Devotion	Spirituality
Morality	Good health	Fun
Family	Freedom	Commitment
Optimism	Open-mindedness	Integrity

Values can come in strings too. A value string is a series of words or other values that define that one value uniquely for you. For example, I have a value string for **Integrity.** I define integrity as being my word, contribution to others, making a difference, playing 100%, service to others, connection, excellence, honor, responsibility, being genuine, learning, growth, and humility.

What would a value string look like for you?

Some other examples are:

Compassion > caring for others > civil rights > standing up for others in the face of difficulty > kindness.

Peace > calm > serenity > being at ease > no struggle > confidence > letting go > not needing to know all the answers.

Of the values (or value strings) you've identified, what do you consider to be your *core* values, that is, the three or four that are most meaningful to you? What values do you live by? What are the values that you couldn't live without and are "universal" for you in all circumstances?

For example, *authenticity* is one of my core values. In honoring this value, I have changed careers from web development/experience design to coaching, allowing me to more fully express my life's personal passion and purpose.

Empowerment is another core value I have. This shows up in how I cheer on my clients in reaching new goals, and as I volunteer as a coach in the community, in addition to doing my very best to live to my fullest potential.

I would be denying these values and doing myself a disservice if I took a job that was uninspiring to me and didn't make a contribution to others' lives in some way.

Now that you've identified some of your core values, ask yourself where they are showing up in your life? Where are they absent?

Values vs. Fear

By revisiting or rediscovering your values, you can begin to see where they are working in your life. Noticing where those values *aren't* showing up is also important. What keeps you from honoring those values? What rules or assumptions have you created for yourself that keep you from honoring those different aspects of yourself? In other words, what are the *fears* that keep you from fully living from your values?

As human beings, we often come across an event or a circumstance where a fear gets triggered somewhere in our lives. Once this fear gets triggered, it usually finds a way to stop us from moving forward. In this place of inaction, we proceed to make a judgment about ourselves. This judgment then becomes a filter through which we always see the world and sooner or later gets into our cells cleverly disguised as a **truth**. This judgment/filter seen as a "truth" gives us evidence everywhere we look that keeps perpetuating the fear, thus keeping it alive.

In coaching, we call these fears "Gremlins." They're also known as your inner voice, the devil on your shoulder, or the committee that keeps you stuck in place. They're very tenacious creatures whose only interest is maintaining the status quo and keeping you from exploring new uncharted territories, that is **change**. For example, a client who stepped into a new job position was confronted with some of the responsibilities she needed to take on to be successful. These new challenges triggered a fear. This fear impeded her in her ability to be organized in setting up appointments accurately to move toward being successful.

She tried different organizing systems and nothing seemed to work for her. When she kept coming up against this perceived failure, she decided that she must be disorganized and irresponsible (self-judgment). When faced with the challenge of being responsible for her own success, her Gremlin created an external excuse (faulty organizing systems) to perpetuate and feed her self-judgment of being disorganized and irresponsible, thus maintaining the status quo and keeping her stuck in a place of inaction. The Gremlin also kept her from looking at the real fear: her fear of success and the responsibility that goes with it.

Most of the time we aren't even conscious of the judgments we are making on a daily basis. We see or experience something, and in the back of our mind we say to ourselves, "see, 'xyz' is so." And when we come across a similar situation we look for proof to substantiate our judgment. "See, I was right!" And as we fixate on an idea, we will begin to see this perspective show up all around us. This self-created "Truth" begins to grow and take on a life of its own.

In the client case above, she started to "see" where she was being irresponsible in different areas of her life. This negative outlook continued to skew her perspective, which then started generating problems in other areas of her life, in addition to her job.

Someone once told me, "Where your attention is, is where your power lies. Where are you putting your attention?" In other words, what you put your attention and energy on starts to show up in your field of vision. This is true regardless of what the thought is. If you are focusing on negative things, then that's what you will notice showing up around you, because that is what you're open to seeing. Conversely, if you alter your view and focus on seeing the positive things, then you'll probably begin to notice the positive aspects in situations and maybe even be pleasantly surprised! Try shifting your perspective in a positive direction for one week and notice what you begin to see in your field of vision.

So look at some of the "truths" you have in your rulebook of life. Are they fears in disguise? What are those fears keeping you from achieving? How could you turn those fears into something that works *for* you instead of *against* you?

My client could have continued down that negative path into a downward spiral, but she didn't. She chose to see a different perspective that gave her a stronger place to stand. One which gave her greater confidence to start reaching for her vision and achieving success.

A new perspective can even help you take those fears and use them to empower you.

For example, a dear friend of mine had a terrible thing happen to her as a child. In that moment as a child, she decided for herself that the world was a scary, unsafe place and she had to protect herself. As an adult, she was able to shift out of her fearful perspective and into an empowering one for herself. She did this by choosing differently. Instead of being motivated by the fear, she chose to be motivated by her values.

From this values-based perspective, she has become a courageous and inspiring women, a mother, and lawyer, who advocates for the rights of children in abusive families. She was able to take her fear, choose differently, and turn it into something that was empowering for her and for the lives of others.

Take some time to review your values. Notice which ones used to be fears in some way and how you've turned them into a powerful place to operate from. Then look to see some of the other fears you have. Where are they stopping you from moving forward? What would be a different perspective you could take that would turn that fear into a value—a value that inspires you to move forward and past the Gremlin to choose differently for yourself?

The Power of Perspective

If you were going to be living your life honoring *all* of your values, what would it look like? Briefly put aside all the assumptions, rules, and responsibilities that your brain is shouting at you right now and just dream for a moment.

- What could you be doing?
- Where would you be living?
- What would you be creating in the world?
- How would your life be?

Write down your answers (without editing it!) so you can see what your heart is saying.

Now, listen to what your Gremlins have to say about those ideas. How loud are they talking? Are they protesting and waving the finger of responsibility at you? They might sound something like, "You couldn't possibly do something like that!" Or maybe, "What about all the other commitments that you have?" Or, "What about....X?" Fill in the blank for yourself.

Write down those answers on a separate sheet of paper. Notice what judgments, assumptions, and rules you've created for yourself. Which ones are "truths" and which are self-limiting beliefs that you've made about yourself or perhaps you've inherited from your family or society? What does this nice box you've created for yourself look like on the inside? Is this how is your life is "supposed" to look?

Now, think about how you can step outside of that box for a few moments and look at the dreams you've written down from a totally different perspective. What do these dreams and visions look like from outside of the box? Is this a perspective that gives you more freedom and more space to express all of yourself and your values? What does this new perspective give you, and what do you see from here? More joy? More satisfaction? More balance?

What would it be like to look at things from this new perspective all the time—this perspective that gives you more *life* and less fear? The great thing to understand is that we're all at Choice about how we respond to life as it shows up. We all have challenging and even difficult things that we have to deal with each day. But we also have the power to choose how to be with it. We are free to choose to be with things in a negative or a positive way and see what there is to see from that place.

What perspective do you want to consciously choose to stand in? What choice is going to give you the view, the freedom, and the satisfaction that you are looking for in your life , your career, or your organization? How would you *like* it to be?

Being laid off from my fancy-titled job was a big blow to my ego and my self-confidence, and left me second-guessing my decisions. But as I carefully listened to my heart for what was really important and what I really knew about myself, a new, stronger place from which to stand began to emerge. I chose to believe in myself again and this new perspective gave me the courage and confidence to inch my way forward into creating a new career for myself.

> "ONE CAN CHOOSE TO GO BACK TOWARD SAFETY OR FORWARD TOWARD GROWTH. GROWTH MUST BE CHOSEN AGAIN AND AGAIN; FEAR MUST BE OVERCOME AGAIN AND AGAIN."
> ~ ABRAHAM MASLOW

Breaking Free

In the Co-Active coaching model that I've been trained in, we hold our clients and ourselves as Naturally Creative, Resourceful, and Whole. What this means is that we each have the answers we need within us.

Have you ever really been determined and committed to figure something out, and the answer seemed to show up? Well, the universe will collude to bring you the things you need and want so long as you're willing to get out of your own way to see it.

If fear is the thing that is standing in your way of seeing your vision and achieving it, how do you get that fear to move the heck out of the way?

Michelangelo once said: "In every block of marble I see a statue; see it as plainly as though it stood before me, shaped and perfect in attitude and action. I have only to hew away the rough walls that imprison the lovely apparition to reveal it to other eyes, as mine already see it."

Try thinking of your vision as the beauty that lies within a rough piece of marble, and your fear is the only thing that is between you and the beauty that lies beneath what the rest of the world sees.

What is the power, the purpose, or the motivation that will enable you to chip away at the fears blocking your view? What is it that drives you and gives you purpose?

Let's go back to your list of values for a moment. What is it about these values that are important to you? How do they motivate you?

My value of empowerment gives me a solid and confident place to stand for myself. It also gives me a sense of contributing to others by giving someone an empowering or inspiring new way of seeing something. Thus helping them remember their own power that they might not have realized they had, allowing them to move forward on their own. I do this knowing that this fresh perspective will make a difference somehow in their life. Making a difference is what motivates me to do this work.

How can you use your values as a catalyst to move past your fears—to blast through them to the sparkling vision that lies beneath those fears?

Christina, a young woman I worked with, is a singer. She's been singing her entire life. She's always dreamed of being a professional singer, but couldn't seem to reach her dream.

Growing up with both of her parents being performers, they always told her "this is no life for you because there's no money in it. It's too hard to be successful as a singer." So as a child, she took her parents' "word" for it. She took their view of the world for her own as a "Truth" and has lived her entire life through the fear and judgment lens of her parents' view of how life is "supposed" to look.

From this perspective Christina could only see "starving artists," individuals who couldn't quite make a living from practicing their art. She could only see the struggle and the hardship.

Instead of following her heart, she took a job in the high tech industry as a project manager "just for a little while" until she could get her singing career off the ground. Well, "a little while" turned into three years working long hours. This "well-paying" job cost her a lot. During this time, her creativity was shut down and she almost stopped singing.

Like many people in the high tech industry, she was laid off from that well-paying, but very stressful job, and took time off. What she found in the space in between was that her value of creating beauty in the world was being almost completely denied. Noticing how she was dishonoring herself and denying her passions, she was able to very clearly understand the cost of her fear. She had let old judgments and fears keep her from what she loved most.

This realization gave her the opportunity to create her own definition of success, leaving behind the one her family had created for her so many years ago. She chose a new empowering perspective from which to see her vision for creating beauty in the world through her singing, her values, and her heart. Her fears are still there, but the Gremlins aren't in control anymore and aren't stopping her from moving ahead.

Christina has stepped fully into being a successful singer and continues to create her vision as she goes, figuring out how *she* wants it to look along the way.

Is there a chunk of marble that's blocking your view?

Some places to consider looking might be:

- Fear of change
- Fear of success
- Isolation or lack of support
- Financial obligations or fear of poverty

- Self doubt
- Family ideals and norms

If one of these (or any other numerous variations on a theme), are in your way of seeing your vision, which of your values can be a catalyst to move you closer to your vision? And if you were to stand in the place of that value, what does the fear look like from there?

Imagine that your fear is the front door of a house. You have a distinct perspective of that door from the outside of the house. Now walk around to the back of the house. The view is totally different. What if you go inside the house, what does it look like from inside? Take the fear that is stopping you and turn it all around, upside down, and inside out to see what it's really made of. Perhaps once you do you'll see it's not as daunting as you first imagined it to be.

Get clear on what's actually the truth about it versus what you've made up. See what there is to move past and choose the path that honors your heart.

Freedom of Choice

There is an awesome power in this choosing. Choosing from your heart, giving yourself permission to actually listen to it, and following through on what it has to say is very freeing. When you begin to choose consciously, it's as if the whole world opens up at your feet.

"WHEN YOU ARE INSPIRED BY SOME GREAT PURPOSE, SOME EXTRAORDINARY PROJECT, ALL OF YOUR THOUGHTS BREAK THEIR BONDS; YOUR MIND TRANSCENDS LIMITATIONS, YOUR CONSCIOUSNESS EXPANDS IN EVERY DIRECTION, AND YOU FIND YOURSELF IN A NEW, GREAT, AND WONDERFUL WORLD. DORMANT FORCES, FACULTIES, AND TALENTS BECOME ALIVE, AND YOU DISCOVER YOURSELF TO BE A GREATER PERSON BY FAR THAN YOU EVER DREAMED YOURSELF TO BE." ~ PATANJALI (1ST-3RD CENTURY B.C.)

With a renewed strength built on the foundation of my values, and the understanding of what my purpose is, I am able to see my vision more clearly each day. I'm able to listen to my heart, trust what it has to say, and choose to move forward through my fears and trepidation.

As I started to map out the details of the vision for creating my own coaching business and began to look at all of the details involved, the fears of scarcity and overwhelm all showed up. But as I kept looking past my fears, my vision became bigger and clearer, like a painting being slowly revealed to its entirety. My vision pulled me forward through my fears, calling forth my higher self to make empowering choices to accomplish all the things needed to make my company a success.

"DESTINY IS NO MATTER OF CHANCE. IT IS A MATTER OF CHOICE. IT IS NOT A THING TO BE WAITED FOR, IT IS A THING TO BE ACHIEVED."
~ WILLIAM JENNINGS BRYAN

What's at Stake?

Starting my company from the perspective of being (happily) unemployed, you can see how getting it off the ground quickly was a big motivator.

As you start to hone in on your vision, look to see what you have at stake. How can you put your vision to work once you've created it? How can you measure it, quantify it, and internalize it, not only for yourself but also for those people who might be working with you. Otherwise is it real, or just some nice, warm, fuzzy thing that you've created for yourself or your organization?

I recently had the opportunity to work with a client and her board of directors on creating a new organizational vision. We took time to walk through and revisit the values that were important to their organization, re-aligned each board member to every one of those points, and from that place, as a team, they were able to create a new vision that resonated powerfully for each of them.

Taking on a new perspective from a much higher vantage point, they created a tremendous shift in how they work together, how they see themselves as board members and as leaders within their organization. A big part of this shift was due in part to how they immediately put it into action and to the test. They could have easily just "tried it on" for a little while before rolling it out to the senior management team, but they didn't. They were willing to dive in feet first, sending ripples of positive change throughout their organization.

They were able to tap into the soul of their organization, clarify the values and meaning of the greater whole, and create a powerful vision from there.

How Do You Find Your Vision?

Finding your vision requires you to look deep inside to see your inner self, identify what your core is made of, and stand from that place to look out at your world. From this solid ground, your perspectives open up, allowing you to see more clearly the fears that have stopped you in the past and move through them, enabling you to see farther than you previously could have imagined for yourself.

Your values give you the mountaintop to stand on where you can see in every direction beyond the fear.

Feel the fresh air, breathe it in deeply, and see what there is to see for yourself, your family, or your organization. From this perspective, the choices are clear and all things are possible.

"BECOME A POSSIBILITARIAN. NO MATTER HOW DARK THINGS SEEM TO BE OR ACTUALLY ARE, RAISE YOUR SIGHTS AND SEE POSSIBILITIES, ALWAYS SEE THEM, FOR THEY'RE ALWAYS THERE."
~ NORMAN VINCENT PEALE

References:

Carson, Richard David. *Taming the Gremlin*, New York: Harper Perennial, 1990.

Kimsey-House, Henry, Phil Sandahl, Laura Whitworth. *Co-Active Coaching: New Skills for Coaching People Toward Success in Work and Life*, Palo-Alto, CA: Davies-Black Publishing, 1998.

About
Michele Molitor

Michele Molitor is a catalyst for change. She is committed to making a positive difference in the lives of others by working with business professionals to explore their purpose and values. To assist them in developing business strategies that reflect these passions and values, enhance their quality of life, and support their personal and professional development.

Trained and certified at The Coaches Training Institute in San Rafael California, Michele uses a holistic approach that integrates your personal and business values with your leadership skills and business strategies to reach greater levels of productivity, success, and satisfaction.

Michele brings passion, commitment, and over 13 years experience to each of her clients. "Throughout my career, I have worked as a consultant, director, manager, designer, and coach for businesses ranging from Fortune 500 companies to start-ups such as UsWeb, Bell South, iPlanet, The Veterans of Foreign Wars, and Global Pathways. My experience gives me a deep well of understanding, business acumen, and creativity to draw upon to help clients identify new approaches to overcoming old obstacles."

Michele coaches executives and independent professionals alike, including writers, musicians, educators, and entrepreneurs.

"I create a safe and collaborative partnership with my clients to help them move past barriers that are blocking their view of what's possible and guide them to achieve extraordinary breakthroughs in development and success."

Key Leadership & Education

- Certified Professional Co-Active Coach, Coaches Training Institute
- Graduate, The Art Institute of Atlanta
- Graduate, Bachelor of Science in Advertising, University of Florida,
- Studies in French linguistics, La Sorbonne, University of Paris, France
- Founder — Nectar Consulting, Professional coaching and business consulting
- Consultant and Web strategist - Global Pathways
- Director of Experience Design – Zefer
- Director of Creative Services – USWeb

Other Highlights

- Member – International Coach Federation, Marin Coaches Alliance, San Francisco Chamber of Commerce, American Society of Training and Development, Bay Area Organizational Design Network
- Affiliate – Innerworks Solutions, Co-leader and coach for corporate coaching programs
- Leader – Co-Founder, Past President, The Interactive Media Alliance, Atlanta Georgia
- Volunteer – Women's Initiative for Self Employment, Landmark Education

You can reach Michele by calling 510.536.9397, sending an email to Michele@nectarconsulting.com or by visiting her at her website, www.nectarconsulting.com.

Live Life More Fully With a Vision

By Linda Snyder

"I've been rich and I've been poor. I like being rich better," was one of my father's pearls of wisdom. My version is "I have lived with a vision and I have lived with no vision. I live life more fully with a vision."

Is your life's vision one of lightness—illuminating your path so that you can see clearly where you are going, helping you get there faster, more confidently, and more joyously? Or is your vision one of darkness—causing you to stumble, fumble, and grope, hiding what is before you, causing you to be unfocused, disoriented, and sidetracked?

You have a choice. Either you are consciously creating your vision, or you are unconsciously allowing life's circumstances to determine your vision for you. Having a clear, compelling vision determines whether you are living with a light shining in your life or you are trying to get somewhere in a fog.

Your vision is a powerful magnet that attracts results that align with the picture you have created in your mind of what you want your life to be like. For example, you have a vision of how you should dress. When you are shopping for new clothes and you look at the various displays and say to yourself, "I cannot see myself ever wearing that outfit," you are being consistent with that vision. You have a similar picture in your mind of what you want for your house, friends, vacations, income, etc.

Look around you. Immediately, you can see what your vision has been for the past five to ten years. Whether you like it or not, your life is a manifestation of what your vision is. Your house, the way you dress, the type of people you associate with, your net worth, where you go on vacation, are all extensions of what you believe your life "should" be like.

What you have been thinking about for the last five years got you where you are today. If you keep extending it out five years from now, you will have similar results in your life unless you do something to change your thinking. No one but you made these "my life should be…" rules. Your life is exactly what you expect it to be.

"Wait a minute," you might say, "This isn't what I want my life to be like." Then why isn't it different? Either you believe it is outside your control and therefore you aren't responsible, or you accept responsibility for your life, but have not made it a "must" to change.

If you passively believe that situations in your life are outside your control and that you are a defenseless raft tossed about in the river of life, you will continue to be carried with the current, never sure of what your outcome will be.

Your Life Reflects Your Thinking

Accepting responsibility that your life reflects your thinking is the first step to living the life of your creation. Nobody else created your life—not your mother, your father, the government, your spouse, your children, your neighbors, or the economy.

One question to ask yourself is "Who role-modeled all the "shoulds" in my life? Most of the time your belief about where you are and how you got there is just an extension of the environment that you grew up in. Your belief system is a combination of your parent's, relative's, and friend's influence, attitudes, and behavior. Whether you play sports or write poetry, went to college or trade school, work white collar or blue collar jobs, your choices determine how your life is lived. You are in your bubble of comfort because of the people with whom you associate, the books that you read, and the TV or movies that you watch. These are the kinds of things that contribute to the image in your mind of what your life should be like.

The next question to ask is "Am I content or dissatisfied with where I am in my life?" All change starts with being discontent with the status quo. Change is difficult. Therefore it is easier to let things be than it is to rock the boat by making a change.

When you reach a point in your dissatisfaction that compels you to change, the "I shoulds" become "I musts." When this happens, the energy shift is tremendous.

This shift in thinking happened to me when I couldn't wear some of last season's clothes. My husband said, "Go ahead and buy the next size up so you will be comfortable." I refused to buy a bigger size, so I knew then that I *must* lose weight. My image of myself did not allow for me to be that size and as a result, I lost 17 pounds and am working toward losing eight more.

When you are at the point that you "must" accomplish something, you are ready to begin creating your compelling vision. There are three steps to creating your vision:

- First, know what it is that you want.
- Second, know why you want it.
- Third, once you are clear on the first two steps, you will know how to bring your vision into your life.

Our local Walgreen store allows me to sort through my finished pictures and discard as many as I want for any reason. As I decide the ones that I want to keep, I sort them into two piles. One includes the clear, crisp, close-ups that give me a positive charge. The second pile contains pictures that are fuzzy, farsighted, or funky.

A clear, compelling vision is like the close-up photos: vivid, clear, colorful, focused, meaningful, and attractive. In addition, close-up photos without a lot of clutter are more pleasing to look at. For example, I was visiting Denali Park in Alaska and took a picture of a grizzly bear on the mountainside. After it was developed, I told friends, "See that spot, over there? That is the grizzly bear." Pictures in a distance do not create any excitement and are passed over in a very cursory manner. In fact, most pictures like that end up in the trash can. Visions that are distant and small usually end up the same way—in the trash can.

When your vision is vague, hazy, and foggy, you will often feel as though you are spinning your wheels. The picture in your mind is fuzzy and because of the lack of clarity, setting priorities is more challenging, getting motivated is more difficult, and passion and creativity are stifled and dormant.

When you create your clear, compelling vision, you will get up in the morning with passion, creativity, joy, and excitement about the picture you have for your life.

Waking up from your sleepwalking state to being fully alive is moving from darkness to light. If you truly want to spring out of bed in the morning, ready to take on your day with boundless energy, the first step is deciding you "must" create your vision and that you and only you are responsible for your vision.

Close your eyes and picture yourself one year in the future. Add five years, then ten years, now twenty years in the future. When you are imagining this picture, what is your health and physical life like? Where are you living? What does your home look like? Where are you traveling? What is your net asset worth?

If you cannot immediately access a clear, compelling vision for each question and each timeframe, then try thinking about it with the end in mind. Say, "Five years from now, this is what I want in my life." Be sure to include all areas. You don't want to have all your focus on wealth and let your health slide. On the other hand you don't want to have health and no money to enjoy it.

Motivations for Change

We have two motivations in our life. One is the "moving toward" motivation and the other is the "moving away" motivation. You move toward things that are pleasurable, and you move away from things that are painful. Both motivations work at different times in your life.

While in Botswana, Africa on a wildlife Safari, we sat with our Guide in the open Land Rover Jeep. A pack of six lionesses sauntered westward on one side of the creek constantly observing twenty gazelles on the opposite side. The gazelles would run forward about a half a mile, stop, and turn to look at the lionesses. The lionesses continued slowly moving forward. The gazelles would wait awhile, then run another half mile and wait. The lionesses were moving toward their pleasure (the gazelles), and the gazelles were motivated to move away from their pain (the lionesses).

Sometimes you are motivated to move toward the pleasure your compelling vision will bring you. Sometimes you are motivated to move away from where you are right now because of the pain you will feel if you don't live out your vision. If you are dissatisfied with where you are now and know you must change, what will motivate you?

What do you need to change to bring about your compelling vision? Is it your finances, your career, or your relationships? Is your motivation the pain of where you are right now or the joy of what you could have? People are motivated in different ways at different times in their lives.

Some of the questions to ask yourself when you are creating a vision are: "Where do you see yourself in the future? Who do you want to be? What do you want to do? What do you want to have? How do you want to live your life? And what would your ideal day, week, month look like?" On which areas of your life do you want to focus: family, career, financial, social, educational, mental, personal, community, health and fitness, spiritual?

What is fun for you? What is exciting, attractive, and motivational? What are you passionate about? What gives you a charge and emotional energy? What causes you to say "Yes" when you get up in the morning and you are excited about what it is that you are doing because you have a passion for it? What is the purpose that you think your life is about? Why are you here? What is significant about what you are doing with your life?

What are your talents? Talent is having an aptitude for something that comes completely naturally to you. There is not a skill that you learned with it. For example, someone who likes to build things as an adult probably liked putting Legos together when he or she was four years old. That is his or her passion and talent. The skill that can be developed by this same person who has a talent for tinkering is to take a carpentry class and learn how to work with power tools. By looking at your passion and your talents, you can begin to see a picture of what you want your life to include.

Whatever we focus on is what we get. You don't get out of life what you deserve or work for, but what you fervently envision. And so when you raise your sights—create a more compelling vision, that is what you will bring into your life. The law of attraction states that we attract into our life what we think about most of the time. And the energy that we give out returns in the form of the answers we receive.

What's Stopping You From Living Your Vision?

More than any other single factor, beliefs stop us from getting what we want, from reaching our potential, and living life to the fullest. Beliefs are the foundation that we build upon, so if your beliefs cause you to be insecure and vulnerable, you must first start by strengthening your foundation.

Picture living in a ten million-dollar mansion with a twelve-car garage overlooking the ocean, with servants and plenty of money. What thoughts go through your mind as you see yourself in that vision? Do you say, "Well I wouldn't want something that big." "I can't imagine something that big." "People that live like that must sell drugs." "I don't deserve that." "Not in this lifetime." "Who needs that many cars?" "Why would I want that big of a house?" "Why not give the money to the poor?"

All those thoughts (beliefs) are preventing you from living in a ten million-dollar house. This is not to say that you need to have that particular vision. However, whatever belief you have about ten million dollars can be asked about a million dollar house, a quarter of a million dollar house, or a hundred thousand dollar house, etc. No matter the amount, your limiting belief about what you see for yourself is stopping you from getting the greatest potential that you can from your life.

Your beliefs produce your life experiences; your life experiences do not create your beliefs. For example, if you believe that all of the people from Mars are greedy and nasty and you walked into a room and there were two people from Mars in that room, you would immediately assume that those are nasty, greedy people. Your assumptions or your beliefs about life, brings those things into reality.

The other day I went to the vet and said "Hi" to a little girl standing next to her father. She turned away and would not say anything to me. Her father said, "She doesn't talk to strangers and people that she doesn't know." In her life, everyone she doesn't know is a stranger; therefore she cannot talk to them.

My son's belief is that everyone is a friend he hasn't yet met. He walks into the grocery store and to complete strangers he says, "Hi, how are you doing." His approach to life will create entirely different experiences than the little girl who believes everyone is a stranger that she should be afraid of.

You cannot bring what you want into your life by focusing on what you don't want in your life. For example, when I talk to my son, I say what I want, not what I don't want. If I don't want him playing in the street and say, "Get out of the street" all he hears is street, street, street. Instead, I tell him what I want: "Stay on the grass."

I don't want you to think of Pink Elephants. What are you thinking of right now? The same happens in your life. When you say, "I don't want to be broke," your subconscious hears "Broke, broke, broke."

Getting what you imagine is a scary thought. You currently have what you have been imagining for a long time. You have a huge pile of bills. What are you saying when you receive those bills? "I'll never get out of debt. All I get are bills. Where does all of the money go? There is never enough." All of these thoughts guarantee that you will get more of the same until you change what it is that you imagine.

Simply by changing what you say to yourself, your results will be different. "I want to have assets worth…" or whatever it is that you want to have your subconscious working to accomplish. Where you put your attention is where your energy goes. Where your energy goes gives you answers to complete your vision.

From "What" to "How" Via "Why"

Thinking about what you want, then immediately thinking of how you are going to accomplish it is a natural transition. When you state that, "I want to…" you will immediately start thinking "How am I going to do that? How can I go from this point to that point? I don't know how I am going to do it."

You slow the process when you jump from "what" to "how." You must add "why" you want your compelling vision. After you have created a picture of what you want in your life, you must know emotional reasons and benefits you want in order to bring your vision into fruition. This step is the "magic" piece that brings tremendous results.

Knowing why you want to achieve your vision is the power that drives its accomplishment. To illustrate, if you drive a bus, the "what" of your vision is the bus, the steering of the bus is the "how" of your vision, and the gas in the tank is the "why" of your vision. Without the gas, the bus is going nowhere, unless it is on a hill in neutral and can coast down the hill. The gas that drives you is your knowing why your vision matters.

The more reasons you have about why you desire your vision, the quicker its achievement. The more emotional (in your heart not in your head) your reasons are, the faster it propels your vision into reality. Imagination is more powerful than the intellect. The more benefits you imagine you will receive, the more rapidly you will enjoy your vision's fulfillment.

The thoughts we think most are what impact our lives in the greatest way. What you think about comes about. Your mind will hold only one thought at a time. You act consistent with your dominant thought. Therefore, it is critical that your dominant thought be about what it is you want to accomplish. There are two similar but distinct ways to do this. One is visualization and the other is self-talk.

Visualizing Your Life

Visualization is a process that imprints and intensifies your future. Your subconscious doesn't know the difference between reality and imagination. The subconscious does not know or understand the concept of time. Therefore, if you create a compelling vision, even though it is in the future, when you bring it into the present, the subconscious goes to work on it immediately. Thus you must convince your subconscious that the condition that you desire already exists. Just as an Olympic champion pictures running across the finish line one thousand times before actually running the race, you are creating your future in your mind.

With visualization you begin with the end in mind. Create a clear mental visualization of your vision as already having been attained. Your description should be sensory rich in detail. How will the accomplishment look, feel, taste, smell, and sound? Include colors, textures, and layers in your picture.

The greater the vividness, clarity, and nearness you can have with your picture, the faster it will come into reality.

Using all five senses, imagine your vision as a reality that has already been achieved. For example, if you desire a new house with a swimming pool, your image might include something like this: "As I walk to the pool, the concrete is hot on my feet. The sun warms my body as I anticipate splashing into the clear blue water. Taking a quick sip of my orange-pineapple drink, I listen to the sound of my favorite music playing on the surround sound system. The breeze rustles through the leaves in the trees and just before I jump off the diving board, I feel complete contentment. I am living in my dream home and am grateful to enjoy my favorite feature, the pool."

Factors that create powerful visualizations are:
- Frequency
- Clarity
- Duration
- Emotion
- Point of View

To start your visualization:
1. Find a quiet place to relax.
2. Get comfortable and think only about the present moment.
3. Access all five senses in your visual imagery: sight, sound, smell, touch, taste.
4. Use your creative imagination to mentally celebrate in advance how you will feel with the end result—the benefits, reasons, rewards, emotions and excitement.
5. Affirm the positive.

Self-Talk

You get what you think you deserve. The results in your life will match your self-esteem. You cannot perform in a way not in alignment with how you perceive yourself.

Therefore, to get better results, you must build belief. Since you have a tape recorder going in your mind anyway, why not ask questions and make statements that will build beliefs that bring the results you want?

With visualization we are creating a clear, vivid mental picture in advance. Visualization imprints images and intensifies those images. Self-talk triggers the mental images you have visualized, and reinforces those images. Self-talk reinforces belief in yourself and that you will reach your goal.

When creating your affirmations for self-talk, choose powerful statements such as "I intend..." "I choose..." "I accept..." "I expect..." "I allow..." "I am ready for..." "I receive..." "I am worth of..." "I am prepared..." "I love..." "I am willing..." "I am open to..." "I am comfortable with..." "I deserve..."

Repeat your affirmations with passion and conviction. W. Clement Stone was a great believer in self-talk and had one main affirmation "DO IT NOW!" along with several secondary ones.

Steps to Developing Positive Self-Talk

The following steps will help you develop your self-talk:
- Decide specifically what you want to do better.
- Affirm the desired behavior as already happening, first person, present tense.
- Include your feeling as part of your affirmation (use feeling words ...ly, ...ing)
- Affirm the positive instead of the negative.
- Affirm only what you truly believe is possible.
- Keep the momentum going by starting each day with positive thoughts.

Do your self-talk and visualization process 15 minutes when you wake up and 15 minutes before you go to sleep. That is when you are in your best mindset to program yourself at a subconscious level. Some people would say, "Oh my gosh, I don't want to program myself." Well you are programming yourself every minute of your day. Did you know that ninety percent of what you think about are your same thoughts repeated over and over? You are programming yourself when you are watching TV. You are programming yourself when you listen to what people are saying around the office cooler. Your environment programs your mind unconsciously, unless *you* are consciously doing something to program your mind everyday.

When you know what it is you want, why you want it, the answers will start coming to you. They come in the shower, on the road when you are driving, when you are doing such activities as gardening, or some kind of repetitive activity that doesn't cause you to mentally have to be totally into what you are doing. The answers to the questions will come, but they come because you have asked the right questions to start with.

Imagination thinks in pictures so you must have something more than just words. Cut out pictures from magazines and create a dream board that has pictures of what it is that you want.

When To Start Creating Your Vision

The clock is always ticking. Nothing is neutral. Everything that we do counts. Everything we fail to do counts. Each choice matters. If you eat high fat, high sugar, low nutrient value food, that might not affect you today. If you do that today, and then again tomorrow, and then continue those same actions for the next week, and the next month, and for a year—you will eventually see the result of that choice and your actions.

The clock is also ticking on your vision. It takes time to create your vision, but this is your life. More people spend time deciding what they are going to wear to the office Christmas party than they do to plan their life. They spend more time planning their vacation than they do their lives. Remember, you are creating your compelling future. Big goals or big visions require big motivations and big energy. Little goals and little visions require little energy.

Sometimes people say, "I am so busy that I don't have time for this and it will make my life busier." What really happens is that having a compelling vision frees you to make the choices that are going to be congruent with your vision. You are becoming intentional about your life, your purpose, your time, and your choices.

The quality of your life has to do with your actions, your attitudes, and your behavior. You continually have demands for your resources of time, energy, and money. Since you have so many demands on those resources, knowing what your vision is helps you decide where you are going to put your time, how you are going to use your energy, and what it is you are going to do with your money. If you want your future to be different, you must behave different, you must think different, and you must act different.

Another very important aspect in creating and then living your vision is that you believe that you deserve to have that vision in your life. Before you can be new on the outside, you must be new on the inside and make room for the new you that believes that you are worthy of living the life of your dreams.

Ask yourself: "If I were to accomplish my vision, what would I believe about my self that I don't truly believe right now? What do I need to believe to have this come into my life? Do I believe that I am worthy of having this?"

About five years ago I was looking through a magazine and I cut out a picture of a beautiful house to add to my dream board. I liked every thing about this house in the picture: the way the light highlighted it, the driveway, the exterior and interior, that it was on a hill, and that it had a circular drive.

Five years later, we were moving to Dallas. I wasn't there

when my husband picked out the house and the first time I saw it was the day we moved into it. The house we live in today is almost identical to the picture that I had cut out of a magazine five years earlier. My subconscious brought it into reality.

What can happen in your life when you have a very clear, specific, and vivid picture of what you want your life, your net worth, your job situation, your promotion, your family, etc. to be? The more vivid your vision, the more precise it is, the more you use your senses, the faster your vision will become reality.

As you consciously create your future, you move from passively accepting life's choices to actively participating in all that life has to offer. As you move from the fog of no vision to the light of a life of vision, you will awaken senses, passion, and creativity that have laid dormant for years. The turning point of living your life more fully will be your decision to create your clear, compelling vision.

About
Linda Snyder

For more than 20 years, Linda Snyder has helped people shatter their self-limitations and break through to higher levels of success. From her humble beginnings of working her way through college as a door-to-door salesperson, Linda became the first woman sales manager and the only person in the company's 100-year history to be sales manager of the year for three consecutive years—a record that still stands.

Through hard work, dedication, and determination, Linda built record-setting sales organizations with publishing and with an insurance company. She has lived the lessons she teaches.

Linda is a professional speaker, trainer, facilitator, and coach with extensive experience coaching companies to grow their business, and individuals who want to do more with their lives. Her expertise is in sales, recruiting, training, managing, and coaching entrepreneurs, business leaders, and self-motivated people.

Linda lives in Southlake, Texas with her husband, Jerry, and children, Chrissy and Reece. To contact Linda you can email her at Linda@LindaSpeaks.com or call her at (817) 424-5725.

A Journey to Re-discovering Your Authentic Self

By Michele Corey

"At every moment you choose yourself, but do you choose your self? Body and soul contain a thousand possibilities out of which you may build many "I's." But in only one of them is there congruence between the elector and the elected, only one which you will never find until you have excluded all those superficial feelings and possibilities of being and doing with which you toy out of curiosity or wonder or fear and which hinder you from casting anchor in the experience in the mystery of life and the consciousness of the talent entrusted in you and the wonder of you which is truly your 'I.' " ~ Dag Hammarskjold

The intention of this chapter is to help you create and carry forth your own vision in ways that successfully translate images into possibilities, intentions into reality, and belief into practices. Remember, vision cannot be forced. It is invited by creating an atmosphere in which all of your ideas can be expressed and honored. Living your vision is a paradigm shift away from acting to a way of being, where you are the cause of your life instead of living because of your life—living from the outside in, reacting to the environment and situations around you and hoping to be happy. Being the cause of your life, coming from the inside out, is a powerful place, full of choice and possibility—a life that honors your core values as being the guiding light.

My coaching business honors the stated intention above by connecting clients to their own clarity, truth, and the magical power of truly knowing self. I recognize and appreciate the fact that there are many methods available for creating your vision, and that there is no single answer. I believe it is important for you to find a process and the tools that work for you. You may completely connect with one specific technique or, like myself, you may be tempted to choose a little of this and that to create your own formula. You'll know when you've found "your" answer. You will most likely feel excitement and it may feel easy or right. You will emotionally identify and connect with what works for you. I often ask my clients to recognize if they feel touched, moved, and inspired by a specific action or outcome. You may want to ask yourself the same question as you continue on your course.

> "IT TAKES COURAGE TO GROW UP AND TURN OUT TO BE WHO YOU REALLY ARE." ~ EE CUMMINGS

When you feel an emotional connection or flow, you will find your self highly motivated and ready to move into action. Coming from a sales and marketing background, I recognize that the emotional connection is the benefit or the reason why we choose to buy something. Unfortunately, what many of us are chasing are the features, or the facts, and for some reason we are unable to figure out why we are not excited.

As an easy example that I often use in my marketing classes, think of a toothpaste commercial for a product like Close Up or Ultrabrite. The manufacturer tells us that the product will whiten your teeth and freshen your breath. These are the facts, the features. Yet what we often see in this type of commercial are two people, often a man and woman in their mid- to late-20's that are frolicking and looking at each other with passion. This is what they are really selling, the emotional connection, the WIFM (What's In It For Me)—or as we call it in marketing—the benefit.

Think about your self. What are your features? And what are the benefits you want to create from the features? We often don't recognize that the reason we make purchases or take action is based on the benefit that is behind the feature. What are the qualities that touched, moved, and inspired you to purchase at least one (this one) and most likely many more self-help books on creating your vision or finding your purpose?

The qualities you list are a key to what motivates you. If you found yourself listing negative qualities, such as "I don't know what I really want," look deeper and ask, "What don't I want?" If you listed something like, "I don't want to feel alone," change it into a positive. What would it say?

"THERE IS NO SCARCITY OF OPPORTUNITY TO MAKE A LIVING AT WHAT YOU LOVE, THERE IS ONLY A SCARCITY OF RESOLVE TO MAKE IT HAPPEN." ~ WAYNE DYER

Can you imagine what it will feel like to create, manifest, and live your dream? You may find that you are like many people who are afraid to take a deep look at what you have created in your present life. There is a poem by Oriah Mountain Dreamer called the "Invitation." I use this poem as a reflective tool during multiple-day intensives with clients. There are two parts that often stand out to clients. At one point Oriah asks you to ask yourself if you are willing to disappoint another in order not to betray your own soul, and the poem ends with the thought, "Do you like the company you keep with yourself in the quiet when you are alone and empty?" To create, manifest, and live your dream, you will find that you must be willing to do both, as well as much more.

I remember the stage in my life in which "finding my purpose" seemed to continually elude me. I read close to 70 books in a year and did every conceivable exercise from values rankings to reflective work to assessments like the Myers-Briggs to non-conventional tools like numerology and tarot. I even wrote a Master's thesis named, *Stepping Stones: The Pathway to Personal Discovery*.

What I most remember about searching for my vision is a conversation I had with a wise woman who told me, "Michele the answer is not out there," she said as she took her hand and waved out into space. "It is within you even now. If you take time to be in the quiet and listen to your heart, you will find it."

At that time in my life I was not ready to hear what that message really said. As you are reading this, you may be in the exact spot I was at that point in my life. And in reflection, I recognize it took many wise women and men to share the same message in their own words before I finally heard the message and put it into action.

"MANY PEOPLE HAVE DREAMS. FEW PEOPLE HAVE STRATEGIES."

~ ANONYMOUS

Unfortunately our lives often seem to be going by so quickly. We are working so hard and fast to do it and be it all, the super mom or dad with the perfect career, the big beautiful house, rearing children that have many advantages. For many of us, we never seem to take the time to focus on what is most important to us in this moment. We think we can start it tomorrow. And, tomorrow soon turns into years.

During this time you may not be aware that your actions are not in alignment with your core self, your values. For example, we say that we value health, yet we rarely take five minutes to sit and be still, allowing our mind to enjoy the nothingness of the quiet. Or, we eat high fat, low nutritional-value take-out because it offers the convenience of time.

While writing my thesis on personal discovery, I read a wonderful article in <u>Fast Company Magazine</u> called, "Betrayal at Work." The bottom line was that even though we may give our heart and soul, there is no loyalty in our workplace. One day when the strategic needs of the company have changed, you may find your self without work, wondering, "How could this have happened to me?" In that moment, the security of the paycheck, the community you built, and the worth you placed in yourself disappeared. I call this living in a flow of non-conscious choice where the words, "I need to," "I have to," and "I should" are leading us to a very non-fulfilling life and business.

Imagine what it would be like to live each day in choice, to personally choose each action you take, instead of doing it because you "should do it." To choose to get up at 6 AM or 7 AM and spend 15 minutes reflecting on what you are grateful for, planning the ten most important tasks you want to complete knowing you are taking at least one action toward your big picture goal, and then moving into action. Living in choice is not about getting up in the wee hours of each day to create a vision and purpose. It's about integrating who you are and what you want from your life, then taking baby steps toward your goal.

What I hope to provide through sharing ideas and reflective questions are some simple steps on the journey to re-discovering your authentic self. Every day, I recognize that by choosing to live the journey and choosing to live in choice, I have grown into my magnificent self and I'm still becoming my magnificent self. In other words, your journey will be constantly unfolding. I have learned how to acknowledge and embrace all of who I am in this moment: the bold, brazen, and magical self, as well as the—at times—fearful and non-confident self. In this dichotomy, I am fully present and aware that I can choose to live in my vision of being bold, brazen and magical, or from my fear.

"IMAGINATION IS MORE IMPORTANT THAN KNOWLEDGE. KNOWLEDGE IS LIMITED. IMAGINATION ENCIRCLES THE WORLD."

~ ALBERT EINSTEIN

Think about what you are currently choosing to create in your life. When is the last time you spent time reflecting upon what you wanted to create, wrote out the steps, and then put them into action? At a recent one-on-one personal visioning workshop, a client said, "I have a very financially successful business. Yet I am so focused on making sure I make enough money and on the business that there's nothing left for me. I feel empty and completely unsatisfied." This takes us back to the choice of either living because of your life (constant reaction to what is around you) instead being the cause of your life and living every day from the inside out, from your values and from your heart. This client doesn't yet see he is at choice to create the life he wants to live. Instead he is unconsciously choosing to allow his business to run his life and the results are his dissatisfaction with both his personal and professional life. Living in awareness is a choice. Also recognize that even when you choose to live in choice it doesn't mean it will always be easy.

Yesterday I was on a client call and the client told me she had just talked with her financial planner and was told that her business was not grossing the dollars that are necessary to provide her with both the lifestyle and retirement she desires. Out of one call she shifted from creating and running a business she loves (coming from the inside out) to focusing on how to make more money. I asked her, "Do you believe that both your current clients and potential clients would both consciously and sub-consciously feel this shift from hiring you because of your passion and expertise, to hiring and working with a person that cares more about how much money is being spent – the constant up sell to increase your bottom line? Who do you believe is most attractive to your current and potential clients?" She paused and reflected back that she realized she was being sidetracked. First, recognize the power and passion you possess when you come from the inside out and your heart (and you can do this in business). Also, recognize those who are your supporters in the life and business you are creating and who are the naysayers that are simply projecting their own fears onto you.

"THE MINUTE YOU BEGIN TO DO WHAT YOU WANT TO DO, IT'S A DIFFERENT KIND OF LIFE." ~ BUCKMINSTER FULLER

As I coach I offer my creative energy, talent, warmth, way of thinking, and expertise. I help people remember why they get up in the morning by challenging them to be aware, explore new horizons, and think creatively about what's now and what's next. My clients say that my enthusiasm is infectious and they love the true collaboration. The gift in our partnership is the brainstorming of ideas, which helps trigger bigger and better ideas. Who do you know in your life that can offer you similar objective support?

"How does one become a butterfly?" she asked. "You must want to fly so much that you are willing to give up being a caterpillar." ~ From Alice in Wonderland.

If you're ready to trigger some bigger and better ideas to help create the foundation of your vision, I offer the following reflective questions to get you started. Remember, give your self permission to dream big and without boundaries.

What is your wildest dream? When answering this question, hold no judgment and know that the sky is the limit. If you could have anything—and neither money nor time is an issue—what would it be? This may be the dream you often think of, or quite possibly thought about when you were younger. If you are having difficulty playing full out with this question, you might want to first ask yourself, "What am I afraid to let go of?" and "What am I afraid to claim about myself?"

What is your realistic dream? This is the dream either you or those around you often think you "should" have.

A quote that had a lot of meaning to me during my "trying to find myself" stage and even now is:

"The opposite of courage in our society is not cowardice, it is conformity." ~ Rollo May

Re-read through the answers to both of your questions. Where are you conforming to the "should" and "have to" statements of life? Where have you not been willing to disappoint another and instead you have either consciously or non-consciously betrayed your own soul? What song is the drum of your soul dying to beat to? Possibly you want to slow down, work fewer hours, and have time for yourself, your family, and friends. Or possibly you find your self caught in a career you never even thought you really wanted, and ten or more years later you don't know how to transition to another one where you would find more passion and still be able to financially support yourself.

"I ALWAYS WANTED TO BE SOMEBODY.
I GUESS I SHOULD HAVE BEEN MORE SPECIFIC." ~ LILLY TOMLINSON

What I recognize in my clients is that they have to give themselves permission to say "No" more often in order to say "Yes" to others. I love the analogy that your life is an energy grid with only a finite amount of squares. And, right now all of those squares are full. In order to get more, you must be willing to do less. That's right. If your grid is full, slow down and focus on what is most important in your life right now. You will want to focus on fewer squares on your grid. You must define which are the most important squares.

"THE INDISPENSABLE FIRST STEP TO GETTING THE THINGS YOU WANT
OUT OF LIFE IS THIS: DECIDE WHAT YOU WANT." ~ BEN STEIN

My business clients often believe that to be more successful they "need" to do more in their business. Then I introduce them to the idea of focusing on the "big rocks."

There are quite a few different stories utilizing the big rocks. This is mine. You are given a bucket and told to put into it big rocks, stones, sand, and water. No matter how hard you try, you are not able to fit all of them in.

The bucket represents what you have chosen to create in your life. Often you will find that you may feel overwhelmed and unable to do every thing that is before you. To have the items fit, you must put them into the bucket in a specific order. First put in the big rocks. In my example, the big rocks lead you toward your vision and goals and must always come first if you want to be successful. In your business these are the Income Producing Activities (IPA's). The big rocks are direct client contact.

The second item put into the bucket is the stones. Shake the bucket and the stones move between the big rocks. The stones represent the activities that form the foundation of your business (the brochures, the marketing plan, the letters). When used with clients they become big rocks, yet the production and management of them are activities that do not produce income. Be aware to not confuse the stones with the big rocks.

The third item to go into the bucket is the sand. The sand immediately finds it place resting between the big rocks and stones. The sand represents the distractions in your business: your friend calling for lunch, the long phone calls with friends and business acquaintances during business hours, the email link that leads you to the internet for 20 minutes, and meeting with what you believe are potential clients that you didn't take time to qualify as not interested in you or your business.

The final and fourth item to go into the bucket is water. The water represents you, your values, and all the intricacies of your life. Notice how easily the water finds it place in the bucket, connecting the big rocks, stones, and sand together. No matter how hard you try, the water will touch each of the items.

Look at your own life. How much time each day do you focus on the big rocks? What would you be able to create if every day you added one big rock that brought you closer to your goals? How would focusing on the big rocks give you more time to enjoy your personal life?

"BY BELIEVING PASSIONATELY IN SOMETHING THAT STILL DOES NOT EXIST, WE CREATE IT. THE NONEXISTENT IS WHAT EVER WE HAVE NOT SUFFICIENTLY DESIRED." ~ NIKOS KAZANTZAKIS

I also recognize that personal growth work is often like a diet. You jump in and see immediate results. Yahoo, this diet is working! Then it happens, that dreadful week where either you plateau or put a pound back on. Recognize that this is part of the process. Notice that as you become clearer with what you desire, your dissatisfaction with the world around you increases. You will notice that you may not like your job or your manager, your significant other is driving you crazy, your house is too small, too big, or too messy. Your friends are so busy they don't have time for you.

This is the "it's all about me" syndrome. If you reread the previous paragraph you will notice that all of the things that are driving you crazy are not about you. Rather, they are ALL about every thing and everyone around you. Interesting! This is when it is time to take a step back and ask your self clarifying questions. What I have noticed about this stage—and trust me we all go through it—is that it can be a turning point where you stop looking outside of your self and start looking inside at what you really want.

As an action, create a list of the things you want to stop doing and the things you want to start. When you look at your stop and start list, what values are you supporting in your life, and what values are not in alignment? If you changed one thing on this list right now, what would it be? How would it help you move toward your goals?

Remember, you are not alone out there. Look for others that have similar values. You can't do it alone. Ask this person(s) to be your support buddy. Set up weekly or bi-monthly phone calls or meet for coffee and create conversation around the things you want to start doing in your life. Have your support buddy help you brainstorm a list of steps and then take one each week. This will help you bring your full self to your dream and the world. You are then living in choice, and you can choose to embrace life and live fully, or act like you don't know what you want.

"...AND THEN THE DAY CAME WHEN THE RISK TO REMAIN TIGHT IN A BUD WAS MORE PAINFUL THAN THE RISK IT TOOK TO BLOSSOM."
~ ANAIS NIN

When your actions are different from what you declare you really want to say or do, you are living your life wearing a mask. The mask has a cost, and the cost is your authentic self. I have been working with a client that recognized he is gay and yet he lives his life as if he is not. I remember sharing with him, "When you wear your mask, some people are going to like you, some won't, and some will be neutral. One day when you choose to take it off you will find that some people are going to like you, some won't, and some will be neutral."

What is the name of the mask you are wearing? Are you pretending to have the perfect relationship or family, pretending to have plenty of money to do what you want while you are drowning in debt, pretending to love your career while you spend many nights complaining and exhausted? How much energy does it take to wear your mask? What is your cost to hide? Where else could you put this energy? What would it bring to your life to be authentically you?

"It's Happening" Alerts

> "WHAT WOULD YOU ATTEMPT TO DO IF YOU KNEW
> YOU COULD NOT FAIL?" ~ ROBERT SCHULLER

I also share with my clients and workshop participants that three "It's Happening Alerts" often show up during the process of creating and living your vision.

The Process is Simple. It seems so easy that you may doubt it will really work. Countless books have been written on how to do X, Y, Z and be successful. You will notice that each one has its own twist. You decide whether this process works for you. What do you connect with? What do you want to change? Remember, it's your vision and your dream. Give yourself permission to change the rules to work for you.

Your Personal Values Show Up. How many of you are entrepreneurs or currently focus most of your energy on your work? Well, then I also want to caution you that even though you may want to only focus on your business, the process of creating your vision also includes your personal life. I guarantee that no matter how hard you try not to involve your personal life, it will still show up. One of the foundational building blocks of your business and professional vision contains your personal values.

Synchronicity Happens. How do you think this one has already showed up? Possibly the fact you are interested in vision and found this book is a good indicator of synchronicity. I can tell you how it has showed up for me. As soon as I chose to do a workshop on creating a vision, people and articles started showing up that supported this topic. I felt flow, and as Joseph Jaworski of the book *Synchronicity* states, it was as if I was "being helped by hidden hands." I love the saying, "When the student is ready, the teacher appears." At that time, it is up to you to recognize the teacher and the lesson.

The Foundation

Vision provides hope of something bigger than you. As many of us have learned, compelling vision may literally save your life. A powerful vision most definitely will enhance your life as well as those around you. Victor Frankl, a founding father of modern psychology, affirmed that the belief that there was something important (a compelling vision) is the most important fact related to overcoming significant odds. Dr. Frankl spent time focused on what enabled some people to survive the concentration camps, while most perished. He concluded that the most important fact of survival was not family background or intelligence, but rather a compelling vision—*believing without a doubt* there was something more important to do.

I remember reading this, and simply sitting still for a few minutes as the weight of it sank in... my senses came alive— touch, taste, smell, hearing, and sight. I kept asking myself, what do I believe without a doubt to be true? Is my own vision that compelling that I could overcome those odds?

Steven Smith, author of *Simple Steps to Impossible Dreams* states, "If you don't have a clear picture of your destination and a precise map to get there, you won't even begin the trip." This is literally looking at "What do I want?"

"ZIG ZIGLAR ONCE SAID THAT MOTIVATION ISN'T PERMANENT. HE WAS RIGHT. MOTIVATION WILL WEAR OFF JUST LIKE SPRAYING YOURSELF WITH COLOGNE WILL EVENTUALLY WEAR OFF. YOU NEED CONSTANT FIXES OF MOTIVATION. BUT, EVEN THAT IS NOT ENOUGH. USING MOTIVATION WITHOUT A GOAL AND A PLAN IS LIKE SPRAYING YOURSELF WITH COLOGNE WITHOUT HAVING A DATE. YOU WON'T ACCOMPLISH TOO MUCH. LEARN HOW TO PREPARE A STATEMENT THAT DESCRIBES EXACTLY WHAT YOU WANT TO ACHIEVE ALONG WITH TWO IMPORTANT FACTORS – WHEN AND HOW." ~ AMAZON.COM BOOK REVIEW OF *THINK AND GROW RICH*

Many of us want to have a vision and goals, yet we don't take any action. I was recently reading Brian Tracy's book *Focal Point*, where he pointed out that only three percent of people actually have written plans that they put into action.

"OBSTACLES ARE WHAT YOU SEE WHEN YOU TAKE YOUR EYES OFF THE GOAL." ~ ANONYMOUS

Brian Tracy also shares how a well-written plan turns your desire for success into an intention. Once you have an intention to succeed, 90% of your perceived obstacles will dissolve and you will have the tools to work with the other 10% as they come up.

Is the following familiar? "I've tried to do a plan. I just can't seem to get it finished. There's so much going on. It takes so much time? Or maybe, I don't really even know what I want?"

The good news is, you've bought this book, and now you've begun the journey to your authentic self. This is the first step. I recommend taking a moment to acknowledge yourself for taking action. Once you begin to think about your dreams, you'll find that defining them can be easier than you think. And guess what, you can have FUN!

I believe the ultimate purpose of a visionary life or business is to transform the world by doing what you love to do. Most true purposes involve service of some kind. I define service as some form of love and some form of positive contribution to humanity and the planet. You may find true success involves personal fulfillment of some kind. I asked my clients and workshop participants to share with me some thoughts and ideas on vision. I believe they may be helpful in clarifying your own vision.

What does having a vision mean to you?

- Focus, seeing what is possible.
- Vision is multi-textured and multi-layered; it involves sight as well as sound and taste and touch and smell.
- Vision gets me out of my bed in the morning.
- A vision can be anything that is a driving force. For example, the smell of fresh coffee causes me to think of its rich taste and caffeinated goodness. I may even see or have a vision of a cup being full, with just the right amount of cream and sugar. That vision drives me to get out of bed and start my day. Any of the five senses can drive a vision.

What makes your vision compelling?

- Vision is my North Star—I chart my way with my vision, to make my time on this earth most valuable to others and myself. Vision is where I focus my energy. It calls me home. It is simple and true.
- Vision is a description of my foundation—identity, values, purpose, prophecy, and mission—that guides me.
- Vision is a guiding light for all decisions, big and small. It has to be memorized, visible, and matching my own values and meaning in life.

What does having a vision give back to you? What did you learn?

- I learned how to be accountable to myself.
- Vision gives me power of choice so that opportunity does not pass me by.
- I find myself excited by the possibilities instead of buried under the weight of the chores.

- Focusing on the big rocks has been the best thing for our (business) growth.

- We learned that we weren't the only ones out there trying to climb this mountain. Michele helped us focus on determining what course of action we needed to take—and setting us off in that direction.

- Vision provided a picture, and pictures are the keys to my intuitive decision-making process—to make decisions that honor my foundation. Clarity of my vision fired up my passion and continues to fuel it.

- Many possibilities open to me and expand when I remain unattached to the outcome of each step, while keeping the beacon of the vision in my mind.

In closing, it is important to understand what part of your vision is continually motivating you to take the next step, and to be aware when fear creeps in. To help you recognize the fear, ask yourself, "What is motivating me right now, my desire to live my vision and my life strategy or my fear?" You can also tell when you have chosen fear over vision because you may be operating in the "I should" or "I have" to do this mode. Or, you may recognize that your actions are not in alignment with what your heart really wants.

What would this situation or goal look like if your vision and strategy were motivating it? What is one step you can take today to move closer to your vision?

I leave you with this quote,

> You are what your deep, driving desire is.
> As your desire is, so is your will.
> As your will is, so is your deed.
> As your deed is, so is your destiny.
> ~ Brihadaranyaka Upanishad IV.4.5.

About
Michele Corey

Michele Corey (formally Chwala) is the co-owner of Advanced Approach, which focuses on personal and business growth strategies. Her approach combines experience from a successful fast track career in corporate marketing and sales with a lifetime interest in self-discovery and growth. Michele draws from her ongoing research and writing to help clients understand the power of utilizing corporate branding on a personal level. She partners with her clients to apply and powerfully communicate both their personal and business value and skills while finding more personal fulfillment, passion, and financial abundance by increasing their bottom line. Her target clients are both individuals and teams that have felt unsatisfied personally and professionally, have the desire to step into the "what's next," and are ready for the journey to creating the results they choose for success.

Michele has a Master's of Science in Management & Leadership, is both a Certified Professional Coach (CPC) and Living Your Vision Coach®. She has her coach training through a nationally accredited school, The Academy of Coach Training. She is also an active member of the International Coach Federation and co-president of the Puget Sound Coaching Association. As a sought-after speaker for her knowledge, down-to-earth wit, and interactive style, you will often find Michele at a variety of organizations in the Pacific Northwest.

Michele loves teaching Sales and Marketing & Visioning Workshops both independently, at the SCORE division of the Small Business Administration, and through The Academy for Coach Training. Michele writes the Coaches Corner, a monthly column in *Verve: A Women's Network*.

Michele often strategically partners with her clients in both a coach and consultative roll for the following knowledge areas: Individual and Group Coaching, Developmental and Process Facilitation, Visioning Work, Sales Management, Marketing, Strategic Planning, Training, Project Management Dynamics, Promotion Development, Managing and Training of third party vendors, as well as New Business and Product Development on both a regional and national level.

Her background includes over nine years experience in Fortune 500 & 1000 companies such as Grand Metropolitan, whose well known consumer product brands include: Pillsbury, Green Giant, Totino's Frozen Food, and Hungry Jack; The Dial Sales Corp, The Clorox Sales Company, and Brach & Brock Confections. In each company she successfully created and executed complex sales and marketing programs with emphasis on bottom line P&L, building business partnerships and generating customer loyalty. Prior to this, Michele worked as a Human Resources Generalist for nearly four years at Della Femina, McNamie, and WCRS, a national advertising agency in Boston, Massachusetts.

Michele believes coaching is an incredible way of helping individuals take responsibility for achieving their potential. When you are ready to fully recognize and unleash your "magic," Michele can be reached at either (206) 525-8709 or michelec@unleashthemagic.com. You can also learn more about Advanced Approach and Michele by visiting www.unleashthemagic.com.

What You See is What You Get

By Vanessa Sandarusi

"IMAGINATION IS MORE IMPORTANT THAN KNOWLEDGE....KNOWLEDGE IS LIMITED, BUT IMAGINATION ENCIRCLES THE WORLD. TO SEE WITH ONE'S OWN EYES, TO FEEL AND JUDGE WITHOUT SUCCUMBING TO THE SUGGESTIVE POWER OF THE FASHION OF THE DAY, TO BE ABLE TO EXPRESS WHAT ONE HAS SEEN AND FELT IN A TRIM SENTENCE... I COME CLOSE TO THE CONCLUSION THAT THE GIFT OF IMAGINATION HAS MEANT MORE TO ME THAN MY TALENT FOR ABSORBING ABSOLUTE KNOWLEDGE." ~ ALBERT EINSTEIN

What if I told you that a personal vision comes *to* you, and not something you have to find? Webster's dictionary defines vision as a vivid, imaginative conception or anticipation. The American Heritage Dictionary records vision as a mental image produced by the imagination. There is no doubt that imagination is the necessary ingredient to develop a personal vision. So let's look closer at what you see and what you will get as you create your clear, compelling personal vision.

Unlike a vision for a business or organization, a personal vision focuses on you and how you see "who" you will be in the future. It evolves in your lifetime as you go through different experiences and increase self-awareness. An organizational vision focuses on groups of individuals and business processes and how they would look in the future. As Dr. Romig states in his book, *Side by Side Leadership*, "A vision is a desirable result to be accomplished by a particular time in the future." A personal vision lacks a specific time expectation and develops from the inside out through introspection and acknowledgement of your God-given natural gifts. An organizational vision is developed from the outside in through stakeholder analysis, business projections, and anticipated future events. Although each type of vision is different, both a strong personal or organizational vision pulls you forward and gives you the validation of why you do the things you do everyday.

A personal vision is that tug within your soul that causes you to change. Creating a personal vision does not require left-brain techniques, like those valued in the business world, and it is not something you push to develop. A personal vision "comes to you" by tapping into your essence. In coaching, we call this focusing on the "who," not the "what" of a person. The "who" of a person is typically explained in some literature by temperaments such as sanguine, choleric, melancholy, and phlegmatic. A coach can help a client identify "who" they are by using standardized assessments, a series of exercises, and using profoundly effective listening skills.

When I work with clients, I listen for patterns when they talk during our coaching sessions. These patterns help me identify "who" they are by how they replicate themselves through speech. To confirm my observations, I would ask my clients questions to clarify what I hear.

In an earlier session with one of my clients, Jan, she talked about her frustrations of dealing with people who are always late for appointments. Jan felt that she kept attracting these people, and she makes a point to let them know that she does not appreciate their lateness. This was an opportunity to clarify a characteristic of Jan that defined "who" she is and I commented, "You seem to have a need to do things on time". Jan thought her sense of timeliness was a value. With further discussion, we were able to discern that it was in fact a need, as it drained her energy when it was not met. This allowed us to develop strategies to address this need of "who" she is when it comes to timeliness and alleviate any unnecessary loss of personal energy.

To start focusing on the "who" of a person in coaching, we begin by looking at needs, values, integrity, and wants. We address a person's needs before we focus on values, because if a person has difficulty meeting his or her needs, there will be a lack of clarity about one's values. Initial coaching sessions would also look at a person's sense of integrity and possibly wants. A person who is getting his or her needs met and has clarity of values can be out of integrity. This can challenge one's ability to move forward and develop a personal vision. Wants are usually addressed to help lead to a clearer personal vision. Lastly, we integrate other techniques that will develop right brain skills that will enhance one's ability with personal vision development and increase the acceptance of the concept that personal visions evolve.

Identify Your Needs

Most of us have heard of Maslow's hierarchy of needs. The bottom of his hierarchy has us needing food, shelter, and water. On an emotional level, coaching looks at needs as those things that if not met, drain you of personal energy. Needs are met by how others behave around you through the setting of boundaries or establishing personal standards. If a basic need that each of us has is not met, there is a sense of disorder and lack of centeredness. Once you discover your basic needs, you will want to develop systems that automatically get those needs met through friends, family, or colleagues.

Let us return to Jan who had a need for timeliness. As a coach, there is no reason to go back in the past to determine why she has the need. We just accept this as a fact and realize that this drains her when it is not met. Jan and I explored strategies by either setting boundaries with others or setting a personal standard for herself. She would set a boundary by letting people close to her know that she will not tolerate lateness. If she makes an appointment with someone and the person is late, she can make it clear that she would leave after a certain amount of time. We played this scenario out further and realized that Jan also cared very much about the relationships in her life. She realized that setting boundaries like this could deteriorate these relationships. We decided to look at strategies that raised her personal standards. These strategies are behaviors that she would take on for herself to get her need for timeliness met. One strategy she tried was to give others 15 more minutes of time needed to meet the appointment. For example, telling them that she would meet them at 1:15 instead of 1:30. Jan always thought about the things she could be doing when she was waiting for someone who was late for an appointment. She now took things she could do in five to fifteen minute blocks of time so she did not feel that she was wasting time. Getting needs met through boundary setting or raising your personal standards like Jan did will allow a person to regain personal energy. This then allows us to focus on clarity of values.

Addressing your needs through the help of others or raising your standards leads to your ability to focus on your values. People's perception of values is generally based on principles or beliefs within a culture. Values can vary from being honest to being service-oriented. We all have natural tendencies of interest that typically evolve in childhood. We later lean toward other tendencies and interests due to our experiences with our environment. Values that are discovered in a coaching setting focus on a person's natural tendencies that lead to the "who" of that person. I like to say that values are almost the same as your God-given gifts as they come naturally to you.

When working with clients who want to identify their true values, I usually have them perform a series of exercises. One exercise is to recall experiences as a young child. What areas of interest did you have at age five or less? For example, I was told that at a young age I loved to carry around books. At the age of two, I would open them and run my fingers across the sentences as if I was reading. I cannot remember if I was reading at that time, but it is no surprise that one of my favorite places to go and relax is in a bookstore. I find that clients sometimes confuse values and needs. In our coaching sessions, we learn the distinction that values come easy for us. A client named, Lisa, easily made friends wherever she went. During our sessions, she would state that people always tell her that she is easy to talk with and get to know. Our exploration of her values revealed that she valued getting to know others and learning. Lisa acknowledged that these were values for her, as it did not take much effort for her to get to know others or learn new things. With these discoveries, Lisa was encouraged to write goals in all areas of her life so that they reflected her values.

Living In Integrity

When clients discover their true values, we are then able to begin working on aligning their life around their values, and look at making sure that they are living a life of integrity. Living in integrity is living a life that is fulfilling and doing what is best for you to make you whole. It is the alignment of your thoughts, heart, and actions. People who have their needs met find it easier to align their life around their values. This can then lead to living in integrity. However, the key to living in integrity is being able to respond to a situation immediately when you are out of integrity.

Most of my clients who have increased their self-awareness of their needs and values have noticed that they were able to respond faster to regain integrity. They do this by reviewing their personal standards or actions that may not reflect their values. I have noticed clients with this increased self-awareness take ownership for everything that happens to them. They begin to make immediate changes to re-align themselves with their values and get back into integrity.

Rita who valued relationships, had a need to be heard. One week she found herself out of integrity at work when she spoke in an unfavorable manner to her boss that negatively impacted their relationship. Because Rita had the awareness of needing to be heard, she realized that something in her life had taken her out of center that caused her to seek getting this need met at work. This typically led to a negative result. Rita started to focus on getting her need of being heard met outside of work by writing in her journal, spending more time with supportive friends who listen to her, and praying more. She found that by getting this need met, she was able to discuss concerns with her boss in a more appropriate manner and rebuild the relationship. This allowed Rita to get back into integrity as her mind and heart valued relationships with others, but her actions that week did not replicate this truth. She realized that something was amiss and was able to respond quickly to make the necessary changes to put her back into integrity again.

Now Look at What You Want

Finally, after addressing needs, values, and integrity, we can look at a person's wants. Most of my clients decrease their level of "wanting" once they address their needs, values, and integrity. We typically address wants as a step to help develop a clearer vision that is compelling. Another client, Lori, was discussing all the reasons she wanted to make a career change. Lori could tell me everything she did not like in her current position. I asked her, "Are you clear about what you do not want in your future career or job?" Lori pondered the question for some time and stated, "Yes." I then asked her to list what she did not want in her future career or job on the left side of a sheet of paper. On the right side of the paper, she was asked to restate what she listed on the left side of the paper into "I want statements." For example, Lori did not want a job where her colleagues gossiped and undermined each other. On the right side of the paper, she wrote that she wanted a job where colleagues valued each other's personal worth and are supportive. The writing of the "I want statements" allowed Lori to see what was possible and led to the development of her personal vision for her next job.

The steps taken to develop a personal vision may be challenging and require some time. Getting your needs met, having clarity of values, living in integrity, and knowing what you want, helps you develop a clearer personal vision that will resonate within your soul. The process will also help decrease distractions and maximize your ability for personal vision development. Your personal vision will come to you, versus having the need to push and develop it.

Using Your Intuition

The premise of this belief is that the vision already exists for you. Your goal is to pull it out of yourself. That becomes easier when you have more clarity about who you are and less distractions exist in your life. The use of intuition helps tap into these untouched resources and leads you to your personal vision. All of us have intuition. Some of us are better at understanding, recognizing, and using that intuition. The use of intuition also helps you respond to the present and allows your personal vision to evolve as you grow and increase your personal experiences and self-awareness.

When my client, Lisa, and I were working on intuition, we discovered how this tool might not be accepted in the business world, where data is required to substantiate a case. I then asked her, "Do you think the higher you move up the organization, that you will have all the information you need to make a sound decision?" Her response was a resounding, "No." Realizing that intuition would help her discover her vision, despite its "unscientific" basis, we were able to explore the development and use of her intuitive skills.

One exercise that I challenged Lisa with was to take five to fifteen minutes out of her day to meditate or clear her mind. She found this exercise difficult, as she was used to being busy every minute of her workday. When Lisa was able to take this time to meditate or clear her mind, she found herself being more receptive to her intuition.

Because intuition appears as if it is magic, and is not based on hard facts, how can you rely on it to make decisions?

I presented a new concept for Lisa to consider when she initially challenged this approach. I asked her, "What if I told you that everything about you has memory? What if I told you that your muscles, including your heart, have memory? What if your brain is not the only storage of memory cells?" Lisa, of course, paused and exclaimed, "Well, I don't know what to think of that. Tell me more." I then talked to her about how our subconscious takes in information that our conscious mind does not realize. When a person uses their intuitive skills, he or she typically has some type of sensation that cannot be explained or put into words. I postulated that this was our subconscious tapping into memory stores not necessarily found in the brain. I also postulated that we take in more information in a single situation than we are consciously aware of, and that our intuition may in fact be that mechanism of tapping into those subconscious stores of information. With that in mind, I also encouraged Lisa to use this skill and to then explore any intuitive sensation by finding tangible information to support her hunches.

This process is not any different than using your conscious awareness of information to make decisions, and then looking up more information to further support it. Using your intuitive skills taps into a larger chasm of information that may not have otherwise been realized. By having Lisa continue to meditate or clear her mind daily, she was able to increase the use of her intuition and begin her final steps toward a personal vision.

As a person becomes grounded by having his or her needs met, and has more clarity of values, lives a life of integrity, knows what he or she wants, and is developing as well as trusting intuitive skills, we can then play with vision development. What might happen to some people is that their vision may come to them immediately. A higher sense of clarity opens up a window of opportunity for a vision to evolve. For other people, it may take some time. A personal vision requires patience and willingness to be open to new things.

Another exercise to develop intuition and right brain skills is to have clients look at play. As adults, we mistake the value of play. Most of us see play as only for children and do not realize its benefits. Play helps develop right brain skills and imagination. Imagination allows us to see things from a different perspective. Play helps increase self-awareness. A personal vision is seeing yourself as you could be, not as you are. A vision is that mental picture of you in the future behaving a certain way and feeling a certain way. It is also based on reality by using skills and knowledge of who you are naturally. Developing your intuitive skills and right brain skills with play leading to creative imagination helps you create a personal vision that is tangible and that resonates for you.

A perfect example of a personal vision and its fulfillment is seen in athletes. Olympic athletes have been known to visualize their performance in their mind over and over again. Having a clear vision of what they wanted to accomplish was found to be the most effective technique to achieve goals beyond the regular preparation of exercise and drills. They required imagination to envision each move they would make as well as consider any obstacles they would face. Many successful athletes who were injured would visualize their technique while going through the recovery process. When they were able to return to their sport, their performance was as good or better than before they were injured.

What if you took time to visualize that vision of yourself in the future? What does your intuition tell you when you play it through your mind? If you have sensations that make you want to run, then are you envisioning something that society or someone else has planned for you? Is it someone else's vision for you? Or does it resonate to your heart and soul indicating that this is the right direction for you, despite what someone else might have to say about that vision? If the answer "yes" comes up with the last question, then you have the right vision for yourself, and you now need to write it down. Be as clear as possible with your vision and make it simple. Most importantly, if the vision resonates with you and is clear for you, it will pull you forward toward achievement. Once you discover your clear, compelling vision, as a coach I would then work with you to fill the gaps from where you are now to where you are going according to your vision.

A personal vision gives you a broad sense of purpose bigger than yourself and your immediate situation. It helps you get through the daily ups and downs of life to justify why you do what you do each day. It validates your everyday efforts to achieve something larger in life that may not have ever been imagined before. A personal vision pulls you forward and makes you make the necessary changes for the future.

Extraordinary people of the past had a personal vision and used imagination to become "who" they are today. They defied any logic and others who did not agree with how they saw things. These individuals range from Albert Einstein to Bill Gates, Abraham Lincoln to John F. Kennedy. These extraordinary people, and others like them, made positive changes in the world. Taking the steps of getting your needs met, clarity of values, living in integrity, and knowing what you want helps eliminate distractions. Developing your intuitive skills becomes easier with fewer distractions that allow you to more readily discover your personal vision. Finally, using your imagination, as past extraordinary people who made a difference in the world did, leads to a clearer creative vision.

So, what is your personal vision? Don't you think it is time to reveal it? What you see truly is what you get. Why not start discovering your personal vision that will make a positive change for others and you? Enjoy the journey to this wonderful self-discovery…you will not regret it.

Take Action Steps

Needs:

1. List all your needs on a piece of paper. Think of a need as something, if given to you on a regular basis, would result in a feeling of being fulfilled and more centered.
2. Narrow down your list to four key needs.
3. Identify 3-4 ways you can get your four key needs met through others or setting standards for each need and then set up action plans to make it happen.

Values:

1. Take some time and think about what you were like when you were a child around five years old and list those things you enjoy doing.
2. Write in a journal for a week focusing on those things you naturally are drawn to and come easy for you.
3. Review your list and journal entries and see if there are trends. What are they? Once you identify the trends, write them down.
4. Review the trends and try to find key words to describe the trends you identified. Did you discover that you are adventurous, analytical, friendly, or mechanically inclined, etc.?
5. Narrow down your list of key words describing the trends to four words. These words will be your values (those things you naturally do and typically are easy for you).
6. Now identify 2-3 goals for each value to make them part of your life again.
7. Establish an action plan to integrate these values into your life on a regular basis.
8. In the future, when making any decision, consider

your values. If three out of four values are not met, ask yourself, is what you're doing worth it?

Integrity:

1. After identifying your values above, list those actions or behaviors you need to change that are not aligned with your values.

2. List other actions or behaviors that keep you from being whole. What are those things that you do that are not aligned with your thoughts and heart?

3. Beside each area where you are not in integrity, write an action plan to put you back in integrity.

4. Start taking action to get back in integrity

Wants:

1. Look at an area of your life where you want to make a change (for example, work, personal relationship, how you look, etc.)

2. List what you do not want in the new situation on the left hand side of a piece of paper

3. On the right hand side of the paper, write, "I want statements" that should be the opposite of the "Do not want statements." For example, if you wrote on the left hand side, "I do not want a boss who micromanages." The right hand side of the page may state, "I want a boss who empowers me to do my job to the best of my capabilities."

Vision:

1. Discovering your vision will take some time if your needs are not met, and you haven't identified your values.

2. If the above steps are completed, and you have a stronger sense of "who" you are, you can now focus on a personal vision.

3. Take some time to do the things you enjoy, or meditate with the *intention* to discover your personal vision. Any flashes of thoughts that come to you should be written down. When something you do gives you a profound, fulfilling sensation, write it down. Do this for a month or two and review your notes.

4. Identify any trends in the information you wrote down. Ask a friend or a coach to review the information to see if any trends are seen. List those trends and start developing a vision for yourself.

5. When writing a personal vision, focus on making it simple. Pay attention to how it makes you feel when you talk about it. Are you full of energy when you explain it to others? If "yes" is the answer, then you are on the right track. If you are less than animated when talking about your personal vision, then go back to the drawing board, relax, and discover what is truly right for you.

Coaching Note: Some people may find that what they are doing today is not right for them and they will need to make significant changes to achieve their vision. Others may come full circle and return to where they began, but with a totally different frame of reference or approach. For example, I had a client who came full circle by trying to leave a specific industry. She later discovered her personal vision is to become an educator to develop future leaders in the industry she was originally trying to leave.

"TIME IS ELASTIC, THE MORE YOU USE IT, THE MORE IT EXPANDS. THE LESS YOU USE IT, THE MORE IT SHRINKS." ~ AUTHOR UNKNOWN

Put time on your side and start discovering your personal vision today!

References

Jones, Laurie Beth. *The Path*, New York: Hyperion, 1996.

Leonard, Thomas J. *The Portable Coach*, New York: Scribner, 1998.

Romig, Dennis. *Side by Side Leadership*, Marietta, GA: Bard Press, 2001.

About
Vanessa Sandarusi

Vanessa has a small part-time coaching practice working with an elite group of individuals who are action-oriented and passionate about making the most of who they are in life. She is the creator of the Extraordinary Living Systems Model used during those coaching sessions. This dynamic model helps clients focus on key areas to reach break through goals.

Clients who work with Vanessa are executives, leaders, business owners, work-a-holics, entrepreneurs, professionals, health care workers, and coaches. Most clients who work with Vanessa seek career development, business development, balance in life, breakthrough goal development, bliss, vision development, and much more!

Vanessa's coaching style is intuitive and pragmatic. Clients enjoy her analytical assessment of situations along with her ability to add fun in the process. Clients will benefit from an array of assessments to gain greater insights. They will also enjoy opportunities to be challenged to speak their truth that leads to "a joyful integrated personal and professional life."

Vanessa is also the founder of the Extraordinary Living Systems Group. The group consists of coaches with diverse approaches with the ultimate goal of enhancing the lives of individuals they work with during the coaching process. You can visit their site at www.extraordinarylife-coach.com.

You can contact Vanessa by email at Elscoaching@aol.com or call her at (513) 769-5421.

Maintaining Your Vision, No Matter What Happens!

By Teresa Aziam

What is Your Dream? Defining Your Vision

High hopes and big dreams have always been a part of my life. While many girls my age were spending time playing with dolls and dreaming of their wedding day, my childhood days were spent drawing blueprints of the dream home I would one day live in, then explaining my vision to my Barbie doll.

That dream house included a waterfall flowing into the swimming pool, an attached hot tub, a deck with a grill and space for everyone I knew, and enough rooms for all my family members. There was a greenhouse on the sprawling back lawn and a long gravel drive lined with towering trees leading up to a circular driveway. The backyard was filled with flowerbeds and small ponds for ducks.

I still want that house, but my dreams have grown through the years and more has been added to the vision: great health, fulfilling relationships, the ability to travel, and the freedom to do it when I choose. Authoring books, public speaking, and leading spiritual retreats are all just a part of what I want for my business. I also want to give back as a philanthropist, give to charities and make a difference in politics. I want to roam to the ends of the earth and back and see sights I can only now imagine. I want to go back to college and study because I *want* to, not because I have to. And I'd like to own a motor coach to travel the country giving talks that provide meaning to me and to the audiences I encounter, and having book signings for the *many* wonderful books I will have written.

What is *your* dream? What delights have been tempting you since childhood? Have you allowed yourself to consider them as anything but a fantasy? Have you shared them with someone only to be mocked or ridiculed, so you stuffed them away where no one, even *you* could find them?

There have been times that I've been criticized for wanting the things I dream of. Nay Sayers attempt to convince me that I shouldn't want so much, or that the things I dream of are materialistic. I don't believe it. And neither should you. I don't worship money or material things; I worship the Great Spirit who assists me in my quest. I also know the value of living my life to the fullest and I realize that it takes money to do so. I've been broke and I've had money—and I can tell you, making a difference and enjoying life to it's fullest is a lot easier with money. Besides, what's it all for if we have to *struggle* through life? That's not living, that's merely surviving.

If you already know what you want, you're a step ahead of most. If you don't know yet, don't worry. Begin to define it right now. Take out a sheet of paper and start writing. Don't judge your list. Don't preconceive reasons why you can't have it. Just write. Write down things from childhood that made you happy. Think about what makes you happy now. Think about what it is that touches you when you watch movies or read books. Is it the character's lifestyle? Is it their friends, their convictions, do they stand for something you want to stand for? Is it their family life, the town they live in, or a combination of these? Do you want a relationship, a home, a car, or a certain body type? Become aware of what makes you smile when the thought crosses your mind. Then make note of what that "something" is. Take a few moments to jot things down that are coming to you now. Free-flow your daydream on paper.

Be Aware of the Beliefs That Affect You

If you're *aware* that you have developed certain beliefs about how your life is, how it should unfold, and what you deserve or what you don't, then you are able to change those beliefs. Being aware of the beliefs that limit you gives you the power to do something about it.

As a child, I heard conflicting messages from family members about what my life may have in store for me. One aunt used to tell me I could do anything I wanted to when I grew up. This was the same aunt who sometimes joked that if I was going to have it all, I'd better marry a rich man. Those opposing ideas caused great confusion, self-doubt, and planted the seed for the belief that maybe I *couldn't* do anything I set my mind to. Years later, I realized I had bought into this belief and that I was unwittingly creating that doubt and fear in my life.

I learned from those around me that life was hard, money was tight, and there was never enough of it to go around. To travel was a "rich man's" pleasure, and since I wasn't rich, I'd likely never do it. *They* hadn't done it, why should I be so different? There are still those in the family who believe I'm just a dreamer. I realized long ago that I could love them and visit with them, but I no longer share my dreams with them.

What are some of the beliefs you have? Take a moment now to list them. Make two columns on your sheet. On the left write down the belief you have now. *"I can't have "xyz" because I didn't come from a family with money; didn't go to college; don't know how."* In the column on the right, write down a new belief: *"I CAN have "xyz" because I believe in it and I'm taking the time to learn it now; because I believe in myself and I have a great support network; because I can find the resources necessary if I choose to."*

Do you recognize the limiting beliefs that are holding you back from your vision? They hide in the shadows and don't want to be noticed. Draw them out and acknowledge them. Once you've discovered what they are, you can decide to replace them. This process won't happen overnight, but if you can find a replacement belief, you can state it whenever you catch yourself thinking in the old way. Little by little you will create a new belief system that will support you.

What Are You Hiding Under That Basket?

Could it be the passion you've been searching for?

Perhaps you're like me and you've had a passion for doing something most of your life. Maybe you've thought it unattainable and have dismissed it as such. Now you feel it creeping into your dreams at night or your thoughts during the day. You feel restless and don't know why. Your job doesn't seem as fulfilling and you can't help but wonder if you're on the right track. You feel as though something is missing, even though you make good money and have a happy family life. Perhaps it's time to allow yourself to reminisce. What was it that you wanted so long ago?

When I was in elementary school, I loved my teachers and wanted to become one. My favorite teacher would read to us everyday and I fell in love with reading and storytelling. That began my desire to write and the dream that one day, I too would be a great author bringing light into someone else's life. I began to write in a journal at eleven and wrote my first book for a school project that same year. I've kept all my journals and I cherish that book!

During high school I abandoned the ambition of teaching. I observed that kids could be unruly little monsters and besides, how would I ever reach my financial dreams on a teacher's salary? The dream to teach was stuffed under the basket to be forgotten.

During my early twenties I was introduced to the world of public speaking. I watched motivational speakers and lit up at the thought that I too, could do that. I loved the way they inspired me and I wanted to bring that to others. I just knew it was for me. But at the time I was too timid to do anything about it and so this dream also went under the basket.

Years passed before I realized that I would only be happy if I followed my heart and began to take my first tentative steps toward realizing my dreams. But I never let go of the hope that my dreams could happen.

Don't Be Afraid to be Where You Are

One thing that held me up, and could be an obstacle for you, is the trouble I had with where I was, compared to where I wanted to be. When I looked at the vast, empty land that lay between here and there, my breath would catch in my chest and anxiety would set in. The space between was too far, too dry, too desolate. I felt I would never make it. I may as well just give up. Why start when I'll just die of thirst, alone and miserable, on the way? Learning how to live with where I was and at the same time not be so afraid of where I was going took some time.

My early twenties weren't easy, and the dream felt more like a fantasy than a possibility. I worked forty to sixty-five hours a week, and yet barely made ends meet. I had no outside support, a lot of bills, and a financial disaster for a live-in boyfriend. I got in deep and began to sink into a pit of despair.

I'd had many jobs of many kinds by my mid-twenties; after all, I had started working when I was fourteen. I knew from the start that working for someone else wasn't for me. I didn't enjoy any part of it, except the paycheck. How could I possibly live like this for the next forty to fifty years?

I wanted more than ever to have my dream career fulfilled, but I was afraid of failing ... which made me afraid to start. And I didn't think I was one of the "lucky ones" I felt set apart from. So I kept my fantasy at a safe distance and embraced and nurtured it only in my dreams. I told myself that one day, when I was ready, I would begin to take action. Maybe I would beat the odds I had perceived for myself. But when I faced myself straight on, I wasn't sure I really ever would. Desire kept me hopeful, but fear kept me prisoner.

Gradually, I felt safe enough to write about my hopes and I began to share my desire with others. At first I chose only friends and family that I trusted would not extinguish the flame. I made treasure maps of my wildest dreams using photos and words cut out of magazines. A couple of them were poster size and tacked to the front of my bedroom door. I began to say over and over again, "One day I will be a famous author and motivational speaker!" And I started to tell anyone who would listen. If I couldn't live the vision right now, by God, at least I would keep it alive. This fostered momentum and spurred me into adding new elements to my vision: a great marriage, a happy family, extensive traveling, and more. I'll explain more about getting there later in the chapter.

Keeping an Eye on Your Intention

Okay, so you've identified your vision, you're aware of your beliefs, you've uncovered the passion and dreams you've been hiding and you've accepted that you must start where you are. Now that you have a cornerstone to start with, what else can you add that will make your life everything you want it to be?

Once I embraced the dream of writing and speaking, I began to add to the vision. The idea of marriage was scary at first. Too many unknowns, a high divorce rate, the risk of losing it all. I thought, maybe I'll just date and find a really great boyfriend. So, several years after a bad break up (with the financial disaster), I began to date again. With each new guy I would discover the things I really enjoyed and knew I wanted in a man if I was even going to consider him for long term. I also discovered a lot about the things I would not tolerate and knew I *didn't want* in a man. I learned not to be too sad when it didn't work out because I believed that if this wasn't the right guy, then an even better one was coming.

I had fun and enjoyed the process. I had so much fun, in fact, that I decided to make it all about the process, instead of concentrating on the outcome. Of course, the process wasn't *all* fun. I had my share of hurts during this time. But because I was willing to risk and to trust, in less than one year I met my future husband, and he was even more wonderful than I had hoped he would be.

This all taught me a valuable lesson in keeping my eye on the intention versus keeping my focus on the expected outcome. If I had expected that each of those prior experiences was going to become *the* relationship, I would have been very disappointed and may have stopped dating long before I met my husband. Instead, my intention was clear—"if this isn't the one, then a better one is coming." I knew what I wanted and I refused to let fear and doubts keep me from it.

Staying with my intention wasn't always easy. Being hurt offered plenty of temptation to give it all up. However, because I decided to endure and trust in something greater than I could see, I got more than I asked for.

Then something interesting happened. I began to see how this principle could be applied in other areas of my life as well.

Do What You Can One Step at a Time

You can't have it all overnight.

By now, you should have an understanding of the process of living your vision. First define it, be aware of your beliefs, stop hiding your dream under a basket, don't be afraid to be where you are, and keep an eye on your intention.

Now for the hard part—realizing that you can't have it all overnight and being okay with that.

You've defined your dream; you're excited, you're ready to go; you're ready for that success **right now**! But it takes time and patience. If you don't have patience, you will give up before you reach your goal. Patience was always a weakness of mine ("Good God man! Will I have to endure this forever? When will the day come when I can live my dream?"). But, I learned to exercise patience by concentrating on one step at a time.

The first thing I had to do was to stop letting fear and doubt keep me from believing in myself. I have always been an avid reader, but I began to pick up the books on self-esteem, dreaming big, and going after what I wanted. I listened to tapes and attended seminars that helped me break through the barriers of self-doubt and old, limiting thought patterns that had me believing I wasn't good enough. And most importantly, I made the decision to start. This might sound simple, but here it is: just start. Start with one area—it doesn't even matter which one because it can be anything.

I learned that if I could do that one thing, I could get to the next step and some day reach my goals. So I started. I signed up for Toastmasters and dove in. It was a small chapter and needed someone in charge of new memberships, so I signed up. Now, not only was I learning to speak in public, I was gaining valuable experience as a board member. Joining the group was the beginning for me and I was on my way.

That one decision gave me the courage and belief to keep going and led me to other experiences that exercised and polished my leadership and speaking abilities. Slowly but surely, I was beginning to realize that I really could get there if I just *didn't give up*.

What can you do today that will set you on your way? Can you write out a plan of action? Will you sign up for that class you've been eyeing? Can you sit down and write the basic idea of what your book will be about? Will you contact that person who can help you if you ask? Can you go to the library and check out some books to guide you?

What you do today will be your benchmark in time. That step will be the beginning. And there is no end without a beginning. Yes, it may be a small thing when you look at the big picture. But how do you eat an elephant? One bite at a time.

Be Your Own Best Balcony Person

Several years ago, Joyce Landorf Heatherly put out a book entitled *Balcony People*. In it she describes the difference between balcony people and basement people. Reading that book helped me to realize that some people are not really "telling you the truth." They are telling you "their" truth and they often think they are protecting you from harm's way by being negative about your ideas, projects, plans, etc. I learned to identify the uplifting, supportive people in my life who I can count on to cheer for me from the balcony, and to identify others who discourage my efforts as basement people trying to pull me down to their level.

No matter what your dream is, you are almost sure to find those folks in your life who are basement people.

I have an aunt who once told me that I shouldn't dream so big because it would only hurt when I failed. She didn't believe in dreaming big. She may have done so when she was young, but her life had not become what she'd hoped for so she stopped dreaming. Her negative outlook was projected onto my dreams and she truly believed that she was protecting me from the hurt she experienced in not reaching her own aspirations.

Those around me have now realized that I am determined and that I dream big no matter what they say. I think I have actually inspired them by holding onto my dreams in spite of the odds or obstacles.

I hold onto my dreams by being my own best balcony person. *I* believe, even when others don't. I nurture the dream by journaling about it, putting up pictures of it, and visualizing it often. I've learned not to share my dream with just anyone. Basement people, or "dream stealers" as I call them, are quick to snatch it away, step on it, or shoot it down. They may even sound well-meaning but they're not to be trusted. Even your friends who swear they support you can be dream stealers in disguise. Their jealousy and envy can distort even their best intentions. My suggestion to you is to keep a very low profile. Try not to tell anyone until it's so strong in you that negative comments or "you can't do *that*" will not deter you. Tell your journal and be you own cheerleader. This is your baby—keep it from harm and negative energy.

Don't Let Others Make Their Experience Yours

How many times have you had a great idea or a secret desire and shared it with someone only to be scoffed at or told that it would never work; they had tried that and it didn't work for them. They had *been there, done that* and therefore you couldn't or you'd get what they got. Remember my aunt. She didn't have the same dreams I had, but somewhere along the way she had convinced herself that the dreams she *did* have could not come true. That was *her* experience, not mine.

Sometimes I would listen to "authority" figures and believe everything they said. They were older and more "experienced." They "knew" more than I did. But, that's not necessarily true. Everyone has their own experiences, their own reality, and really it's based on their beliefs and circumstances. Just because they had a certain outcome or they *think* that's what the outcome will be based on their beliefs, doesn't mean that's what will happen. Be careful not to invest heavily in what others tell you. This is not to say their words should not be taken into consideration. Perhaps they have a valid warning that should be heeded, or a piece of information that could save you time and money in your endeavor. My advice to you is to always run what others tell you through your own filters. I tell this to my clients when we first get started: if the advice you're hearing doesn't feel right to you—take what does and leave the rest. There is no one person out there who knows everything. Nor do they know what's right for you. Part of this journey is learning how to trust your own advice and deciding what's right for you. Sometimes the journey can feel lonely and scary. I sometimes wish that someone could just tell me what choice to make when things get difficult. They can't. You could ask fifty people and they would all have their opinions, but at the end of the day, it's you who must choose, you who must live with the consequences. Learn from the experiences of others, but most importantly learn to trust your own experiences.

Be Proud of Your Dream

Do you have a tendency to feel self-conscious talking about your dream? Do you feel like you're bragging? Do you think others won't respect it or understand it? Do you downplay your dream when speaking to others so they won't think you're trying to be *all that*?

This might be another reason not to talk about your dream with others who may not appreciate it. However, feeling uncomfortable talking about it can also be a gauge for you to determine how you really feel about your dream. If you really don't believe in it yourself, you'll sound that way to others. If you're afraid that they will think you a braggart, maybe you don't want to share it with them because they're not safe to share with. Or maybe you aren't able to claim the idea of success for yourself.

When I talk about my dreams, I glow. My whole being lights up and I relish the thought. It shows! And even if others aren't normally excited about writing or public speaking, they get excited to see me so animated about my passion. I'm proud that I have decided to go after my dreams. There's no feeling like it. I know there will be obstacles to overcome and challenges to face, not to mention long hours, sleepless nights, and lots of learning, but the rewards are already outweighing those obstacles.

Keep Going. Even If It Seems Like It Will Take Forever to Reach the Top

At one time, I was under the false assumption that the people I saw living their dreams had always been successful, or at least found success easily once they knew what they wanted. I thought there was something wrong with me because I knew what I wanted but it wasn't coming fast enough.

Now I know that it takes time. The length of time it will take each of us is different and cannot be predetermined, even if we think we know how long it *should* take. Becoming discouraged and quitting is tempting. Selling yourself short by thinking you don't really need or want that—how about something else that's not so hard to attain?—is easy. *Don't!*

Keeping focused and staying the course has taken me years to perfect. I've read books, played tapes, and searched the Internet. I've interviewed others who have what I want, who have been to seminars, workshops, and classes of many kinds. You may not do all that I've done, but be sure that if you're serious about succeeding you'll take that first step! You see, once the decision to go for it is made, that's it. Every time you are in a position of choice from then on you know you have two options—the one that will take you closer to your dream, and the one that won't. Attaining your vision isn't always easy and it isn't always comfortable, but you make progress step by step and one day there you are. I'm not where I want to be ultimately, but I'm content knowing I'm so much closer than I was last year, last month, or even last week. That only comes by never giving up the dream. If you maintain the vision no matter what—you won't be disappointed. Of that, I *am* sure.